אַךְ שָׂמֵחַ

Ach Sameach

אַךְ שָׂמֵחַ
Ach Sameach

Lessons from the Jewish Holidays

Compiled by
Menashe R. Frank

Copyright © 2017 Compiled by Menashe R. Frank

First printing

Paperback ISBN: 978-1-947341-09-8
eBook ISBN: 978-1-947341-08-1

Library of Congress Control Number: 2017957315

All rights reserved. No part of this book may be used or reproduced by any means, graphic, electronic, or mechanical, including photocopying, recording, taping or by any information storage retrieval system without the written permission of the publisher except in the case of brief quotations embodied in critical articles and reviews.

A collection of *divrei Torah* about the *parashiot* is available in a first book, compiled by Menashe R. Frank, entitled Attah v'HaLevy v'HaGeir.

DEDICATION

This *sefer* is dedicated in honor of

Rabbi Edward Davis

הרב אליהו מאיר בן זלמן ברוך הלוי שליט״א

Please see page ix

This *sefer* is dedicated in memory of

Jeanette Levine

חיה יאכעט עלקא ע״ה בת ר׳ ישראל יצחק ז״ל

Please see page xii

CONTENTS

ix	Dedication: HaRav Edward Davis by Menashe R. Frank
xii	Dedication: Jeanette Levine ע״ה by Josh Levine
xix	Approbation
xxi	Acknowledgements
xxiii	Notes, Disclaimers, Apologies and Conventions
xxix	Preface
1	Introduction by Jamie C. Frank
11	Jamie's Family Photos
19	Yom Tovim

Rosh Hashanah 21
Yom Kippur 31
Sukkot 43
Shemini Atzeret 55
Simchat Torah 63
Chanukah 71
Purim 83
Pesach 97
Shavuot 115
Tisha B'Av 131

139	Calendar Converter
141	Glossary of Terms, Places and Persons
161	Sources and Influences

DEDICATIONS

HaRav Edward Davis
By Menashe Frank

יְהוֹשֻׁעַ בֶּן פְּרַחְיָה אוֹמֵר, עֲשֵׂה לְךָ רַב, וּקְנֵה לְךָ חָבֵר

Yehoshua ben Perachia says,
"Make for yourself a rabbi, acquire for yourself a friend . . ."
—Avot 1:6

A great rabbi was once traveling from town to town by wagon. Wherever he went he was greeted with great fanfare and honor by the townsfolk, who lined up to ask him questions. As time went by, the rabbi's wagon driver became frustrated and impatient. Finally, he mustered the courage to ask the rabbi "Why is it that you are received with such honor everywhere we travel? I do not see why you are so deserving! I could answer all the questions the people pose just as well as you can. It is only because I am driving the wagon that no one pays me mind." The rabbi calmly considered the driver's grievance and proposed a solution. "If you would like, I will switch places with you for a day," said the rabbi. "I will drive the wagon and you can speak with the people." The driver was enchanted with the idea and immediately accepted. As they approached the next town on their journey they exchanged clothing and the driver took up position in the rear of the wagon with the rabbi now driving up front. Sure enough, the townsfolk greeted the driver as if he was the famed rabbi, pouring adulation upon him. But before more than a minute had passed, the first person presented the driver with a complex and difficult question of Jewish law. The driver quickly realized he was wholly unqualified to provide any answer at all. Trying not to panic, he sagely stroked his beard and passively declared "You call this a question? It's really quite simple! Why even my driver can answer this question . . . ."

The truth is that being the Rav of a large Congregation is anything but simple. And not everyone is cut out to be such a leader. Rabbi Davis is legendary in the Modern Orthodox Jewish world, having shepherded the Young Israel of Hollywood/Fort Lauderdale from a membership of less than fifty families in 1981 to more than 600 by 2017. Clearly he possesses the superlative skill, intelligence, wisdom, patience and demeanor to bring about dramatic and positive, large-scale communal results. Yet the relationship that our family has with Rabbi Davis is a very individualized and personal one. Simply put, without Rabbi Davis our Jewish life would not be possible.

My wife Jamie and I were introduced to Rabbi Davis in 1996, and the story of his involvement in my conversion and his facilitation of our Jewish journey is detailed in the <u>Introduction</u> to my first *sefer* <u>Attah v'HaLevy v'HaGeir: Lessons from the Weekly Torah Portion.</u> It is fair to say that without the benefit of Rabbi Davis as our "referee" during our adoption of a *Torah* lifestyle, Jamie and I might not have made it through the process. He expertly guided two strong-willed individuals with disparate growth rates and differing "religious baggage," keeping us focused on the goal, encouraging us to compromise, and all the while keeping the atmosphere light-hearted and positive.

The *Mishnah* states "עֲשֵׂה לְךָ רַב, וּקְנֵה לְךָ חָבֵר. . . ," "make for yourself a mentor, and acquire for yourself a friend." (Avot 1:6) This is commonly understood to mean that one should first choose a rabbi and then, inevitably, the rabbi will become his friend. While Rabbi Davis and his family have certainly become the dearest of family friends over these last twenty years, I would suggest an alternative reading of the *Mishnah*. By virtue of finding the right rabbi, one is able to preserve and enhance his relationship with his greatest friend: his wife. (see Malachi 2:14) Because of the tremendous love and respect we each have for Rabbi Davis, Jamie and I were able to defer to and accept his judgment concerning the myriad of issues that inevitably arise in building a Jewish home. By making Rabbi Davis our Rav, we became the best of friends!

We join with the rest of our Hollywood Congregation in congratulating Rabbi Davis on his recent retirement. We will be forever grateful for all that he has done for our family, and we are confident that, G-d Willing, our precious relationship will continue and grow in the years to come.

Jeanette Levine (1958-2009)
Chaya Yachet Elka bas R' Yisroel Yitzchak, a"h
(5719-5770)
By Josh Levine

On November 12, 2009, after a hard-fought, relentless, years-long battle against a rare form of cancer, my mother was taken from this world at the young age of fifty-one. Menashe and Jamie came to my parents' house shortly after they heard the heartbreaking news. I hugged Menashe for a good while, and we cried on each other's shoulders. It was a very sad day, but, on some level, it comforted me to know that Menashe and Jamie truly appreciated and felt everything we lost that day. At my mother's levayah later that night, I eulogized my mother along with three other people: Rabbi Edward Davis, our beloved, longtime shul Rabbi and very close family friend; Rabbi Kalman Baumann, an esteemed Rabbi and educator for whom my mother had profound respect and with whom she worked for nine years; and Menashe. In his eulogy, Menashe explained that if he had to encapsulate my mother's essence in a single word he would describe her as "regal." As Menashe expounded, she conducted herself as a *bas Melech* because she understood that she was a daughter of *Hashem*. Menashe's concise description was unequivocally correct.

My mother—Jeanette Levine, Chaya Yachet Elka[1]—was born and raised in Miami Beach in the home of my grandparents, Isidore, Yisroel

---

1 My mother was named after two relatives on her mother's side, Yachet and Elka, both of whom were great women who were tragically murdered during the Holocaust. My mother gave honor to those great women who preceded her. We hope that our daughter, Chaya Yachet Elka ("Elki"), possesses the wonderful traits of her Bubby and continues to give honor to those names. It is also a true testament to my mother, and the special relationships that she developed with the Wittlin and Davis families, that non-relatives Rabbi and Mrs. Gabi and Rena (Davis) Wittlin named their oldest daughter Chaya Yachet Elka after my mother.

Yitzchak (ע"ה), and Anne, Chana Rochel, Himelstein. A book could easily be written on their *emunah* and *bitachon*, love of *Torah*, quality of character, sincerity, and acts of kindness. To this day, my Bubby dedicates herself to *chesed* and *tzorchei Tzibbur* with the energy and vigor of someone half her age. May she be blessed to continue to do so *ad meiah v'esrim*. I am certain that growing up with my Bubby and Zaidy had a large part in enabling my mother to become the unique person she was.

My mother met my father, Norman Levine, in the home of my mother's best friend at the time, Debbie (Goldring) Zisquit in Miami Beach.[2] My mother got engaged to my father at the young age of seventeen, as a senior in high school, and got married at the age of eighteen. But her maturity far-exceeded her age. As a teenager, she envisioned the family she intended to build and raise, and she brought her vision to fruition together with my father. Although my father was not brought up in an Orthodox Jewish environment, he embraced the spirituality that my mother and the children brought into his life.

Over the years, my father and mother together helped to educate and inspire others about the beauty of Orthodox Jewish life. In fact, several people currently living in the Hollywood Community would tell you that the *Shabbos* and *Yom Tov* meals at my parents' home—including the delicious food, very meaningful discussions about *Torah* and Jewish philosophy, and, of course, the lighthearted and hilarious conversations (mostly with my father)—and their respective relationships with my parents were crucial components in their decisions to become *baalei teshuvah* and

---

[2] Reena—my youngest sister and only sibling not married at the time my mother passed away—started dating in the spring of 2011. She went out with a few boys but had not yet found the right match. In the summer of 2011, Debbie Zisquit decided to call Reena with a *shidduch* suggestion: her youngest son, Jonah. In one phone call, she set up her son with a magnificent young lady and loyally looked after her best friend's daughter to set her up with an exceptional young man. They got married in the summer of 2012. Needless to say, when Rabbi Davis spoke under the *chuppah* to share the history and *Hashgachah Pratis* leading up to the marriage and to guarantee everyone that my mother was dancing at the *simchah*, it was quite difficult to find a dry eye in the room.

live lives of *Torah* Judaism.³ Two such people are Menashe and Jamie. Menashe sent the following handwritten note to my parents after his first *Shabbos* meal at my parents' home:

Dear Friends –

What can I say? My Shabbat meal at your home was phenomenal! It strengthened my resolve in my conversion process, and gave me innumerable examples of exactly why I am doing this. You made me feel like family, and I am so very grateful.

See you soon & thanks.

שלום

Chris

When I was young, my mother had a successful stationary business called "Innovative Invitations by Jeanette," but the advent of high-tech computers and email forced her to find another occupation. She then worked in the Toras Emes Academy of Miami office for nine years, during which time she constantly expressed what an uplifting and fulfilling experience it was to work for Rabbi Baumann and the other administrators and teachers, in a school she loved and admired. Rabbi Baumann delegated responsibilities to her that he had previously handled himself because my mother was highly competent and possessed excellent judgment. For those very reasons, Menashe was determined to recruit my mother to

---

3 An attorney named Robin (Dubowitz) Andisman became a very close student and friend of my mother during the years she was learning about Orthodox Judaism. Robin essentially became a part of our family, and she considered my mother to be her mentor and role model. During the years Robin dated, my mother provided ongoing encouragement and told her that she would eventually find her *bashert*. Our entire family was delighted when Robin finally met Joe Andisman, and we were thrilled when they decided to get married. Unfortunately, my mother's illness had progressed by the time Joe and Robin got married, and my mother was unable to attend the wedding. Feeling that her presence was so sorely missed, at the conclusion of the wedding, Joe and Robin insisted on visiting my mother at her home. They left the wedding hall in their wedding attire, brought a video of the *chuppah* recorded earlier that night, and watched it together with my mother. Joe and Robin brought the wedding to my mother because they knew it was truly her *simchah*, as well.

work with him at an enterprising new company called MAKO Surgical Corp., where he served as General Counsel. He offered her a generous compensation package, which presented her with a substantial dilemma: She enjoyed working at Toras Emes and felt that the environment was spiritually elevating, but she also felt a strong responsibility to contribute to her family's financial wellbeing.

This was an incredibly difficult decision for my mother, but after careful consideration and Rabbinic consultation—both of which were typical of my mother's approach to important decisions—she decided to join MAKO. When she joined, it was still in its infancy. She played a large part in taking the company public and became a valued and respected member of the team. My brother, Marc, later joined MAKO and had the opportunity to work with my mother. Marc knew that my mother was proud to see him grow professionally, but Marc took <u>more</u> pride in observing my mother in the work environment. He described my mother's delightful, professional, can-do attitude amidst all the challenges present in the corporate world, and he never saw her compromise her principles, regardless of any social pressures. Simply put, she made a *Kiddush Hashem*. Unquestionably, working with Menashe was an incredible opportunity for my mother because—aside from sharing many detail-oriented tendencies and excellent work ethic—they shared the same unwavering commitment to their principles.

My mother developed unique relationships because she was a true *chaveirah tovah* to her family and friends. Those who had the opportunity to speak with her about personal matters will likely recall several distinctive aspects about her ordinary approach (which was not all that ordinary) to those conversations. My mother would provide an attentive listening ear, would respect the confidentiality of the matter, would express compassion and empathy, and would most-often come up with some rather insightful advice. She would usually encourage, empower, and provide an optimistic perspective; and she did not merely share feel-good advice but always incorporated *Torah* values and her nuanced appreciation for sensitivity in interpersonal relationships. Talking to her was truly a unique experience.

In the weeks after my mother passed away, my remarkable wife, Gitty, mentioned to me that she always felt comfortable sharing her thoughts and feelings with my mother and wanted to hear what she had to say. She felt completely safe and secure talking to her, and she looked upon my mother as a pillar of strength and courage. In part, this was due to the fact that my mother possessed a uniquely high level of emotional intelligence, but, in part, the trust, confidence, and comfort we felt when speaking with her stemmed from knowing the type of person she was. We knew she was constantly working to improve herself and was guided by what she believed was the *Ratzon Hashem*. We knew she was not swayed by social pressures; she was independent, sincere, and consistent. As a result, she earned the profound respect of her husband, children, and so many of her friends up until her very last day in this world.

It was apparent that my mother had developed great *emunah* and *bitachon* in *Hashem* from the way she conducted herself throughout her life, but these *middos* were on full display toward the end of her life. From the time she became sick, she never once expressed any anger. She dutifully underwent all the necessary medical treatments, mindful of the fact that *Hashem* was capable of healing her if He so desired, but, incredibly, she accepted the fact that *Hashem* may make a different choice. She never lost faith or trust in the *Ratzon Hashem*. At my mother's *shloshim* ceremony, Marc shared the following story:

> On what would be the last morning of my mother's life, I came to the house early to be with Mom and relieve my brother of his all-night shift. I tried communicating with her, but I wasn't very successful, as her condition didn't allow. I was frustrated. I got my guitar and I started to sing, hoping I would get a small response like the days prior, but I didn't get much. I continued anyway. The last song I sang was "Ani Ma'amin," "I believe," the words from the first of the "Shalosh Esrei Ikarim," "the Thirteen Principles of Faith." In English, the words mean: "I believe with perfect faith that *Hashem* is the Creator and Guide of everything that has been created and that He alone has made,

does make, and will make all things . . . ." So I sang the verses, "Ani ma'amin b'*emunah* shelaima, sheHaBorei yisborach Sh'mo . . . ." And then I began to sing the chorus, and, as though it had been rehearsed, on cue, Mom began to sing! "Hu Borei Umanhig l'chol ha'bruim." That was all her energy would allow, so I finished the chorus: "V'Hu l'vado u'suh, v'oseh, v'ya'aseh l'chol ha'ma'asim." Two hours later she passed away—but not before that final declaration of faith."

My siblings—Marc, Shira, and Reena—and I came to the realization that, growing up, we took much of my mother's character for granted. As Marc aptly put it, "When I was younger I innocently thought that every adult 'gets it'—that it's just a matter of time and of growing up. And when we do, everyone ultimately acquires wisdom, sensitivity, a keen sense of right and wrong, integrity, devotion, good judgment, tact, love and affection, *emunah*, *bitachon*, and a growth-oriented mentality . . . . But then I grew up, and realized that these attributes that my mother obtained are not the default; they aren't given. These extraordinary qualities come with years of personal work, refinement, and character development."

As the classic *mussar* work, Mesilas Yesharim, explains in his introduction: "The foundation of saintliness and source of pure service [of *Hashem*] is that it be clear and true to a person what his obligation is in this world." My mother had that clarity of vision and that focus because she truly worked on herself to obtain it. She learned *sefarim* and read secular books on growth, and she underlined, highlighted, and took notes. She assessed her growth. And she constantly strove to learn and grow more. She worked to improve her *emunah* and *bitachon*. She worked to improve her character. She worked to improve her marriage. She worked to improve her parenting. She worked to be *miKadaish Shem Shamayim*. She worked to become a true *eved Hashem*. And she never lost focus.

My mother saw in Menashe and Jamie a couple who embodied the desire to learn and grow—and learn and grow they did. Menashe and Jamie saw in my mother a "regal" *bas Melech* who loved them and taught them both in the literal sense and by example. I am sure that this special occasion, Ayden becoming a *Bar Mitzvah*, and the publication of this beautiful *sefer* are a source of great *nachas* to my mother and that she is celebrating along with the Frank family.

Mazel Tov! May we be blessed to share many more *simchas* together.

APPROBATION

בס"ד

הנני בא't בזה להגיד של הספר "והיית אך שמח"
שנלקט ונוסף ע"י הרב מנשה שאול פרנק נ"י א'
וראשים שונים בעניני שמחה בתורה. ודיסק גמרא ומצוות ומעלות
חסמים כראוי.

הספר הזה הוא לקוטי דברי תורה ופרפראות של האומרים
והוא שלים את הספר "אתה הלוי" והראשי הכל
בדברי תורה של פרשת שבוע אחת כנה האחד הב' ויורד
איחד הכל משימים על דבר השכ ושמחה.

עברתי של כל הספר ונהניתי מאוד של החידושים היצאים
בו וראוי לכל משפחה, לעורר עניין ולהגיע לשמחה של כל
אחד בהכל.

התכלית יש לן כח ויכלת לקנוץ ולהבין ולהרגיש עוד
פרטים אחרים.

בכות התורה. וזכן ולוי וזל כל משפחתו. וירבה רוח
נחת מנכדיו. ויחי' חיים של שלום ואהבה. ושמחה.
התקוה. יברכנו וישמחי בכל טוב. ויזכה לראות וזרבנו
בכל אשר יפנה. וזכה כולו לגאולה שלימה מהרה
ב'אמן

בברכת התורה.
כהנים בן איישנתן
שליט

BS'D

I present this letter as acknowledgement of my approbation of this *sefer* Ach Sameach, which was collected and printed by Menashe Shmuel Frank, who is G-d fearing and who sets aside time to learn *Torah* and whose commitment to *Torah*, *mitzvot* and *chesed* is exemplary.

This book is a collection of *divrei Torah* and insights on the yearly holidays, which complements the author's previous book Attah, v'HaLevy v'HaGeir, dedicated to the *parshiot* of the year. Together, the two books offer *Torah* insights for every *Shabbat* and holiday.

I reviewed the book in its entirety and found it to be enjoyable and enlightening. It is a book that is worthy to learn every holiday and rejoice in its deep thoughts.

Hashem should give Menashe merit and strength to create and publish many other *sefarim*. The merit of this book should shield him and his family, and bless him with abundant *nachat* from his children and a life of *Torah*, peace and joy.

May the Al-Mighty bless the author with all good. May he merit the blessing "He will bless you on all your endeavors." We should merit together to see the Redemption soon in our days. Amen.

With blessings of the *Torah*,
Rabbi Chesriel Yosef Jankovits
Av 5777/July 2017

ACKNOWLEDGEMENTS

As with my first *sefer*, the *hakarat hatov* I have for being able to compile this second sefer begins and ends with *Hashem*. "הַלְלוּקָהּ אוֹדֶה ה' בְּכָל לֵבָב בְּסוֹד יְשָׁרִים וְעֵדָה" "Hallelukah, I shall thank *Hashem* with all my heart with the assembled Congregation of the righteous." (Tehillim 111:1)

The Sources and Influences list sets out the eclectic roster of people who contributed, in most cases unknowingly, to the content of this book. I am indebted to each and every one of them for sharing their words of *Torah*, first with me, and now with a broader audience.

Mrs. Suzanne Jacoby Offer and Rabbi Keith Wasserstrom were indispensable in proofreading and editing the *Yom Tov* chapters. As with the first *sefer*, I could not have compiled a book of this nature and scope in the days before the ArtScroll revolution in Jewish learning and while we were all saddened to hear of the recent death of ArtScroll co-founder Rabbi Meir Zlotowitz ה"ע, we gratefully acknowledge the enormous impact he had and will continue to have on world Jewry. Torah.org and Chabad.org are two superlative Web-based *Torah* resources that were hugely helpful. The very talented Sara Stratton of Redwood Digital Publishing was again the steady hand in guiding me through the second book publishing process. Most importantly, my *Rebbe*, Rabbi Yossi Jankovits, employed his encyclopedic knowledge of *Torah*, *Gemara* and all secondary sources to ensure this book met the same exacting standards as the first.

This *sefer* is about the *Yom Tovim* and the holidays are about family. Each of my children, Yael Rani, Esther Miriam, Binyamin Pinchas and Ayden Avraham are unique and amazing contributors to the diversity and richness of our family. Although this book is being published in celebration of Gidge becoming a *Bar Mitzvah*, each of our children independently makes us "ach sameach."

And finally, "אחרון אחרון חביב," "the very last is most beloved," (Rashi on Bereshit 33:2), I want to acknowledge and thank my beloved wife Jamie, who not only tolerated the publication of a second *sefer*, but actually crafted its Introduction. "רַבּוֹת בָּנוֹת עָשׂוּ חָיִל וְאַתְּ עָלִית עַל כֻּלָּנָה," "Many daughters of [Israel] have done well, but you have surpassed them all!" (Mishlei 31:29)

NOTES, DISCLAIMERS, APOLOGIES AND CONVENTIONS

This Second Book

This *sefer* is the second effort I have made in compiling *divrei Torah*. The first book, Attah v'HaLevy v'HaGeir, was published in 2015 on the occasion of my oldest son, Binyamin Pinchas, becoming a *Bar Mitzvah* and provided insights into the weekly *parashiot*. This *sefer*, celebrating my younger son, Ayden Avraham, becoming a *Bar Mitzvah*, offers perspectives into the Jewish Holidays. Thankfully, the enormous amount of work that went into producing the first *sefer* could be leveraged for the creation of the second. For instance, the first *sefer* included many *divrei Torah* about the *Yom Tovim* which were appropriate for republication in this second book. Also, many of the components of the first book (e.g., the Glossary of Terms, Places and Persons, and the Sources and Influences) were duplicated and updated for inclusion in this *sefer*. Even this Notes, Disclaimers, Apologies and Conventions section is generally drawn from the first book since the basic points apply equally to the second book.

The Yom Tov Chapters

More than twenty years ago I began compiling the *divrei Torah* set forth in this book. The intention was to include annually one entry per

Yom Tov based on something I heard or read during that year. I provide the Hebrew year in which each entry was recorded, and have included a Calendar Converter to assist the reader in connecting an entry to the corresponding year in the Common Era.

During the time I was compiling these entries, my understanding and appreciation of both the substance and process of *Torah* learning advanced. In the early years, I would sometimes capture a concept without identifying its source. I ask forgiveness from those I inadvertently omitted, yet are deserving of credit for teaching me. In compiling this book I had to make judgment calls and adopt conventions of uniformity. For example, I have avoided applying my limited and deficient judgment concerning proper titles for attributed Sources and Influences, and therefore have listed all male religious figures as "Rabbi" (rather than Rav, HaRav, Rosh Kollel, etc.) and, in the case of women, "Rebbetzin." I intended no disrespect and ask for *mechillah* for any offense. Occasionally, where a source himself used an appellation other than Rabbi to quote another, I have included that alternative title (for example Rabbi Edward Davis, and many others, often referred to Rabbi Soloveitchik as "the Rav").

There is an entry for each *Yom Tov* for most years, although in some years there is no entry and occasionally I made more than one entry in a given year. The only criterion for inclusion was that the *Torah* thought struck a chord with me to the point that I wanted to retain it and draw inspiration from it again and again.

Significantly, I have included *Tisha B'Av* as a *Yom Tov* chapter. I did this for two reasons. Firstly, there are important inspirational lessons to glean from *Tisha B'Av*, which occurs in the summer months when we are sometimes less attentive to *Torah* ideas. Having an easy reference by which to connect to this important fast day may prove helpful to some readers. More importantly, the inclusion of *Tisha B'Av* is a hopeful recognition of the *Hashem*'s promise to turn our current fast days into *Yom Tovim*. "כֹּה אָמַר ה' צְבָקוֹת צוֹם הָרְבִיעִי וְצוֹם הַחֲמִישִׁי וְצוֹם הַשְּׁבִיעִי וְצוֹם הָעֲשִׂירִי יִהְיֶה לְבֵית יְהוּדָה לְשָׂשׂוֹן וּלְשִׂמְחָה וּלְמֹעֲדִים טוֹבִים וְהָאֱמֶת וְהַשָּׁלוֹם אֱהָבוּ," "So said *Hashem* of Legions: The fast of the fourth [month], the fast of the fifth [month – *Tisha B'Av*], the fast of the seventh [month], and the fast of the tenth [month] shall be for the house of Yehudah for joy and happiness and for happy holidays-but love truth and peace." (Zechariyah 8:19) May it occur speedily and in our times. Amen.

Our family often spends *Sukkot* in *Eretz Yisrael*, where *Shemini Atzeret* and *Simchat Torah* are celebrated on the same day, and this is reflected in the entries for those holiday chapters. While I have included a separate chapter for each holiday, there is obvious thematic overlap, and both chapters should be relevant to each separate day as celebrated in the Diaspora.

I struggled with the inclusion of *Pesach* in a *sefer* that I hope will be utilized regularly at the festive meals of the other *Yom Tovim*. Obviously, a *sefer* exposed to *chametz* year-round should be used with the utmost caution on *Pesach*.

In a few places I note *halachot* connected in some measure to the *Yom Tov* at issue. While in all cases these *halachic* notes were gleaned from the teachings of my Rabbis (usually Rabbi Edward Davis), they should not be relied upon as authoritative.

In a few cases I include my own original *Torah* thoughts, sometimes as an addendum to something I heard, occasionally in the form of a question, and in a few isolated instances, as a free-standing thesis. This is indicated by the insertion of "MRF Note" in the text. Where I took what I believed to be any kind of a step out onto the proverbial theological limb, I always tried to check with a *Torah* authority (usually Rabbi Yossi Jankovits) to ensure the idea was genuine and in keeping with normative Jewish thought. In the handful of cases that I presented him with an original *Torah* idea, I cannot recall even a single time that Rabbi Jankovits showed less that complete enthusiasm for my *chiddush*. While some unattributed entries may have been my original thought, I only claimed the ones about which I was certain.

On occasion I included personal political statements associated with both Israel and the United States and connected in some way to the *dvar Torah*. I do not intend to offend those who have an alternate perspective.

Verses from *Tanach* are presented first in Hebrew and then immediately translated to English. A portion of a verse is occasionally presented in transliterated Hebrew, followed by the English translation. For readability, Hebrew words and phrases are transliterated, italicized and defined in the Glossary of Terms, Places and Persons.

I routinely capitalize Hebrew and English words that I feel are deserving of that respectful treatment. This includes reference to *Hashem* and any Aspect of Him, but is extended to words such as, for example, Holy, and references to the Land of Israel and the People of Israel or to the Sons of *Yaacov* and Brothers of *Yosef*. I tend to use the Hebrew names of personages (e.g. *Moshe*) rather than the English version (i.e. Moses), but I do provide the English names in the Glossary.

Many of the *divrei Torah* were originally presented (and often recorded) with *Ashkenaz* transliterated spelling of Hebrew words (e.g. *chanukas habayis*), but I have made most defined words transliterated in the Sephardic pronunciation for uniformity (i.e. *chanukat habayit*). There are exceptions, however, where certain words just sound more natural to me when presented as pronounced in the *Ashkenaz nusach* (e.g. *bris; Shabbos*), or when used by my dear friend Josh Levine in his moving Dedication to his mother, ע"ה. The same convention also applies to Sources & Influences (see below).

Glossary of Terms, Places and Persons

Entries are transliterated (as best as can be) from Hebrew, and occasionally Yiddish or Aramaic, and alphabetically ordered without regard to spacing or punctuation within words or phrases. Entries for which there is both a singular and plural form are separated by a "slash." For entries that are often, but not always, accompanied by another word the second word follows in parentheses (e.g. *Yosef (HaTzaddik)*).

The definition provided is limited to assisting in understanding the use of the word or phrase in the context in which I present it. Alternate but inapplicable definitions are generally not included. Dates are Hebrew years unless designated with CE or BCE. Hebrew months are reckoned from *Nissan* (with the reckoning from *Tishrei* in parentheses).

Sources and Influences

Entries are presented in alphabetical order based on what I understand to be the most accepted appellation for the source. Accordingly, for example, Rabbi Yisrael Meir Kagan haKohein is presented as the Chofetz Chaim, the name of one of his *sefarim*. Where a source is identified as a *sefer*, it is italicized and the author, if known, is provided. Most sources are presented in transliterated Sephardic pronunciation (e.g. Daat Zakainim), but there are notable exceptions (e.g., Chasam Sofer) based on how they best sound to me. Only very basic information about each source is provided (e.g. years of life, geographical connection). I have not begun to do justice to the greatness and accomplishments of many of the sources and I ask for *mechillah* for my failure to do so. I encourage each interested reader to do additional research on the personages listed.

Male non-rabbinical sources are called "Reb," or, if applicable "Dr.," neither of which should be read as judgment of individual erudition, which in some cases rivals the Rabbis. For the most part I did not include any honorifics for deceased sources (e.g. alav hashalom; ע״ה; ז״ל), so as not to draw comparisons between individuals. Of course, it is my desire and prayer that those whose teachings are set forth in this *sefer* and who are no longer with us should draw merit from their posthumous contributions.

Finally, at the time Attah v'HaLevy v'HaGeir was published, the United States Supreme Court rendered its dishonorable decision in Zivotofsky v. Kerry, striking as unconstitutional the law passed by Congress requiring the U.S. State Department, if requested, to list Israel on U.S. passports as the country of birth for Americans born in Jerusalem. With the arrival of the Trump administration in Washington has come renewed hope that the United States, along with other foreign powers, would recognize Jerusalem as Israel's capital and take diplomatic steps consistent with that recognition. However, *David HaMelech* instructs us clearly. "'טוֹב לַחֲסוֹת בַּה׳ מִבְּטֹחַ בָּאָדָם, טוֹב לַחֲסוֹת בַּה׳ מִבְּטֹחַ בִּנְדִיבִים'," "It is better to rely on *Hashem* than to trust in man; it is better to rely on *Hashem* than to trust in nobles." (Tehillim 118:8, 9) The Vilna Gaon (Mishlei 14:26) explains that even unwarranted reliance on G-d is more productive than the explicit promises of the nations. *Hashem* has promised His People that Jerusalem, or, more properly, *Yerushalayim*, is and shall remain the undisputed, undivided capital of the Jewish State, regardless of what those in Washington or anywhere else might say or think. Accordingly, any reference to *Yerushalayim* in Sources and Influences is clarified as being in Israel.

This book contains the holy Name of G-d in Hebrew. Please treat it with respect and dispose of it properly.

PREFACE

וְשָׂמַחְתָּ בְּחַגֶּךָ . . . וְהָיִיתָ אַךְ שָׂמֵחַ

And you shall be happy on your Festival . . . and you shall be completely/ only happy!
      —Devarim 16:14, 15

יָדַעְתִּי כִּי אֵין טוֹב בָּם כִּי אִם לִשְׂמוֹחַ וְלַעֲשׂוֹת טוֹב בְּחַיָּיו. וְגַם כָּל הָאָדָם שֶׁיֹּאכַל וְשָׁתָה וְרָאָה טוֹב בְּכָל עֲמָלוֹ מַתַּת אֱלֹקִים הִיא

I perceived that there is nothing better for [man] but to rejoice and to do good during his lifetime. Indeed, every man who eats and drinks and enjoys what is good in all his toil, it is a gift of G-d."
      —Kohelet 3: 12, 13

Rabbi Yitzchak Salid points out that it is extremely unusual, especially *chutz l'Aretz*, for the *parshiot* of Matot and Maasei to be read on separate *Shabbatot* during the summer months. Rabbi Ephraim Greenblatt provides a fascinating reason as to why our Sages established the calendar to require that Matot and Maasei be combined. There are three *Shabbatot* occurring during the *Three Weeks* of sadness when we lament our myriad National catastrophes, including the destruction of the First and Second Temples. Our Sages determined that Parashat Devarim must be read on the third *Shabbat* which immediately precedes *Tisha B'Av*, at the end of the *Three Weeks*. That leaves two *Shabbatot* during the *Three Weeks*, and our Sages further ruled that, in most years, Parashat Matot and Parashat Maasei must be read together on the second *Shabbat* on the *Three Weeks* in order to ensure that Parashat Pinchas is read of the first. What is so intrinsically important about Parashat Pinchas that necessitated that it be read during the *Three Weeks*?

Rabbi Greenblatt explained that all of the *Yom Tovim* of *Am Yisrael* are described in detail in Parashat Pinchas, which is a required consolation to our Nation during the *Three Weeks*. Of course, we must recall with sadness the horrific events that occurred during this period throughout our history, but we must temper our sorrow by recalling the happiness we will experience with the conclusion of the *Three Weeks* and the onset of our annual holiday season. In fact, Pesikta d'Rav Kahane states that just as we are despondent in the summer months when where are no *Chagim*, we are downhearted in the *Three Weeks* when we are bereft of our *Batei Mikdash* and the ability to bring our National *korbanot*. The first *Shabbat* of the *Three Weeks* is therefore a propitious time to read about the *Chagim* and *korbanot* as set forth in Parashat Pinchas, to kindle a joy that will ultimately manifest in the greatest happiness when *Mashiach* arrives and all National fast days, including those of the *Three Weeks*, become National *Yom Tovim*. (Zechariyah 8:19)

It is hard to argue with the Sages on this point. Anyone who has experienced the annual cycle of the Jewish holidays can attest to the meaning and magic contained in each *Yom Tov*. The *Yom Tovim* are the precious milestones by which we measure our Jewish lives. They are times when family is the priority, when delicious food is served in abundance, when our gratitude to *Hashem* is overflowing, and by which we re-energize our spiritual existence for the purpose of continually increasing in our closeness and service to our Creator. In short, the *Yom Tovim* make us happy, and that is a gift from G-d.

This *sefer* is the sequel to <u>Attah v'HaLevy v'HaGeir: Lesson from the Weekly Torah Portion</u>, which was published in 2015 on the occasion of my oldest son, Binyamin Pinchas, becoming a *Bar Mitzvah*. In the <u>Preface</u> to the first *sefer*, I describe how over the many years following my conversion, I took it upon myself to record, on a weekly basis, an interesting, provocative or inspirational *d'var Torah* related to the weekly *parashah*. I did the same for every *Yom Tov* as I experienced it, and, in hindsight, the entries demonstrate a progression in my *Torah* outlook over that eighteen-year period. Those handwritten notes eventually filled an entire three-ring binder, which I regularly reviewed and augmented. My notes on the *parshiot* were published in <u>Attah v'HaLevy v'HaGeir</u>, and my entries on the *Yom Tovim* form the content of this book.

My first book not only provided insights into the weekly *parashiot*, it included an <u>Introduction</u> that described in detail the unique Jewish journey undertaken by Jamie, my wife, and me. That story, which centered around the shocking revelation by my paternal grandmother, ע"ה, that she, my deceased father, ה"ע, and their entire family were Jewish, was understandably yet undeniably focused on the Frank side of our family. What was missing was Jamie's voice, by which she could relate the Cohn family history as well as her perspective on how she came to adopt a *frum* lifestyle in her adulthood. Thankfully, with the publication of this *sefer* entitled <u>Ach Sameach: Lessons from the Jewish Holidays</u>, Jamie has ably crafted her own <u>Introduction</u> that tells her story with the perfect mix of nostalgia, honesty and humor.

Finally, a word about the title. The *pasuk* which includes the *mitzvah* to be "ach sameach," "totally [or only] happy," (Devarim 16:15) comes from Parashat Re'eh, and is specifically describing the *Yom Tov* of *Sukkot*. Yet it is juxtaposed to the *Torah's* description of the *Shalosh Regalim*, and the *Gemara* (Pesachim 109a) understands that *Simchat Yom Tov* applies to all the *Yom Tovim*. There is a double entendre at play, however, for "ach sameach" describes not only the required perspective of *Yom Tov* but the natural disposition of our dear son Ayden Avraham, who is now becoming a *Bar Mitzvah*, in celebration of which I am publishing this *sefer*. Ayden is a perpetually happy person, demonstrating a positive zest for life that irresistibly draws people to him and which makes him a joy to be around. Undoubtedly, he acquired this superlative *middah* from his mother. May *Hashem* bless them both, along with our other children, our extended family, our dear friends and teachers, our precious Hollywood Jewish Community and all of *Klal Yisrael*. May we together merit the coming of *Mashiach*, when we will all be "ach sameach," and celebrate together in a rebuilt *Yerushalayim*, and may it be soon, speedily and in our days. Amen.

M.R.F
Summer, 2017 (5777)

INTRODUCTION

וְהוֹלַכְתִּי עִוְרִים בְּדֶרֶךְ לֹא יָדְעוּ בִּנְתִיבוֹת לֹא יָדְעוּ אַדְרִיכֵם אָשִׂים מַחְשָׁךְ לִפְנֵיהֶם לָאוֹר וּמַעֲקַשִּׁים לְמִישׁוֹר אֵלֶּה הַדְּבָרִים עֲשִׂיתִם וְלֹא עֲזַבְתִּים

"And I [Hashem] will lead the blind on a road they did not know; in paths they did not know I will lead them; I will make darkness into light before them, and crooked paths into straight ones. These things, I will do them and I will not forsake them."
—Yishaiyah 42:16

I was once asked to speak at my daughters' Modern Orthodox Jewish high school. Yael, our oldest, was a junior and Emma was a freshman. When I was contacted by the event coordinator I assumed she was simply inviting me to attend a mother-daughter(s) event. Unlike my husband, I had never before been asked to speak publicly about my Jewish journey, so I was completely unaware that they actually wanted me to be part of the program meant to inspire the girls between *Rosh Hashanah* and *Yom Kippur*. The coordinator explained that there was to be three presenters: me and another mother who, like me, was a *baalat teshuvah*, and one mother who was a convert.

I checked with my girls to ensure they wouldn't be embarrassed. While they had many times heard their father's fascinating story recounted publicly, this would be the first time that the story would be told from my perspective and point of view.

One of my closest friends was incredulous. "Why would they ask you to speak? What could you have to say?," she asked in genuine disbelief. Truth be told, I was secretly asking myself the same question. In all the years of telling the story of how Menashe and I became religious, not many people asked about my "story." I was looking forward to speaking to the girls because I thought I had something valuable to share with them.

Nearly all of the women and students present that day were significantly more skilled in their Hebrew and knowledge of their Judaism than I, even though I was in my 40's and had already been "on the plan" for more than fifteen years. I did undergo a *"Bat Mitzvah"* ceremony at age twelve in my Reform "Temple," where I read from the *Torah*, yet these high school girls at age fifteen and sixteen were light years ahead of me in knowledge and abilities. I would never be able to catch up.

Growing up in Tampa, Florida, I had actually attended an Episcopal elementary school, which was the best school within walking distance in my neighborhood. There wasn't a viable Jewish day school option at the time. A start-up school with ten kids in each grade was struggling to get going, and was never a consideration for my parents. Instead, my formative school experience included going to weekly church services and learning the Christian prayers and hymns through osmosis. As one of the few Jewish students I never kneeled or took the communion, but for eight years I certainly was exposed to more Christian ritual and dogma than Jewish.

I was forced by my parents to attend weekly Sunday School at my "Temple." I didn't know very many of the kids and I was completely lost, no matter what was being taught. Perhaps, I had no interest, perhaps I couldn't relate to something that we rarely talked about at home. I had one Jewish friend from Sunday School whom I hardly ever saw, for she lived on the other side of town. Otherwise, all my closest friends growing up were gentiles.

While not at all religious, my parents, Douglas and Maureen Cohn, whom I have always adored and admired tremendously, were very involved in the Tampa Jewish Community through secular organizations such as UJA/Federation, AIPAC, Israel Bonds and JNF. They held prominent positions at Federation, and were always chairing committees, raising money and encouraging their friends to get involved. They were whole heartedly committed to those organizations with their time and money. Through their example, once I left home for college and for years after graduating, I too became involved in these same organizations. To remain "Jewish" my parents constantly reminded me that they expected me to marry a "nice Jewish guy." Their only Jewish expectations of me were to give time and money to the Jewish Community and marry a Jew.

I would never criticize the way my parents brought me up. I had an amazing childhood. My parents gave my older brother and me so much love and support. They are truly my role models and my closest companions and advisors aside from my husband. Their *middot* are stellar and their generosity is endless. They have mentored so many young friends and professionals and even volunteered to assist retiring military personnel to help them reengage in civilian life. These are all character traits that were passed on from their parents and grandparents. And even though they are not directly tied to *Torah* learning, I believe they acquired the best characteristics from their prior Jewish generations who did live lives of *Torah* observance and learning.

Our family was very fortunate. We were largely unaffected by the Holocaust because both sides of my family had been in America since well before even the first World War. My paternal grandmother's family was the last to come from Russia in the early 1900s. If there were distant relatives that were still in Europe during the *Shoah*, it was never made known to us by the previous generations.

My parents grew up in Omaha, Nebraska, where most of my extended family was also raised. They were brought up with Midwestern values such as hard work and patriotism. My father served in the Army Corp of Engineers, thankfully in the lull between the Korean and Vietnam Wars. Success in my parents' eyes was to move out of their small town and provide a better lifestyle for their children. Being culturally, but not religiously, Jewish was very important.

So we made our life in Tampa, where there were few Jewish families scattered throughout the city, with whom we would occasionally interact.

There were always two or three Jewish kids in every grade at St. Mary's Episcopal Day School, Berkeley Preparatory School and H.B. Plant High School. Following my *Bat Mitzvah* celebration, my Judaism was a twice a year event: on *Yom Kippur* we would fast and go to "Temple," and on Passover we would make a *seder*.

Our lives changed dramatically when my older brother Greg decided to become completely immersed in *Chabad Lubavitch*. He had gone off to University of Pennsylvania a nice, sweet prep school graduate and returned to Tampa a kamikaze *chasid* intent on observing *Shabbat* and converting our home to a kosher kitchen. Needless to say, I was not happy about the ensuing disruption in my decidedly non-Jewish lifestyle and aspirations of being a debutant and selected to the Junior League once I graduated from college. The stark contrast of how he left home and how he returned was rather traumatizing to me, which laid the ground work for some of my very deep-rooted irritations with Orthodox Judaism. Within two years, I myself left for college, which afforded me the opportunity to once-again ignore my religion.

It wasn't until after college, when I started dating Chris Frank, that the events of my childhood became relevant to my life. The particulars are set forth in (mostly accurate) detail in the Introduction to my husband's first *sefer* Attah v'HaLevy v'HaGeir. In a nutshell, Chris was the Catholic boy I promised my parents and myself I would never date. We had dated briefly in college, and even though I became more and more serious about my requirement to marry a Jewish guy, there was always something pulling me towards him. I certainly tried to dissuade him at first. I told him we could only be friends. I even set him up with my Catholic friend from home. But once we started dating it became unavoidable. I only kept saying I would never marry him unless he converted to Judaism. How he accomplished that was, for me, not important.

The result of all that is well known. Chris became Menashe through an Orthodox conversion and we were married in the Orthodox tradition. Yet I was still far from connected to *Yiddishkeit*. When my brother asked if he could say one of the *Sheva Berachot* under the chuppah at the wedding, I was appalled. Firstly, I had never heard of such a thing as "Sheva Berachos," (as I am sure he pronounced it), and secondly, anything done under the *chuppah* would be done by the cantor, whose operatic voice would boom majestically throughout the ceremony. I had never heard of a lay person saying anything under the *chuppah*. I eventually gave in and let him say one of the blessings, completely unaware that this is how all Orthodox weddings are conducted. I know now that it is the biggest honor to say one of the blessings for the bride and groom. Little did I know that my wedding experience would merely be the beginning of the humbling experience of unearthing my complete religious ignorance.

Menashe was convinced that we needed to move to Hollywood, Florida, where Rabbis Edward Davis, Rabbi Howard Seif and Rabbi Seymour Atlas ל"ז had converted him, and where Norman Levine and his dear wife Jeanette Levine ל"ז had taken us under their wing to basically raise us in the world of Orthodox Judaism. To put it bluntly, I was NOT interested. I didn't want to join in the fun and I was functionally illiterate regarding Judaism. I didn't know what a *shul* was, or what *Shacharit* and *Minchah* were, or even the difference between a *Siddur* and a *Chumash*! I couldn't even remember the names of the Levine girls, Shira and Reena, two names so different from the Kristens and Teresas that I knew from my Tampa days. The only thing I could manage was trying to learn the rules of keeping *kashrut*, *mikveh* and *Shabbat*. And even with that, I didn't know what I was getting myself into. In the beginning, I was on my own. I thought I was brilliant in purchasing all red dairy utensils and all blue meat utensils. I had no idea that the entire kosher world had adopted a system that was actually the complete opposite!

Eventually Menashe convinced me it would be the best thing for us to move to Hollywood. He begged me to trust him and take a chance. When we moved, I wanted to settle on the far outskirts of the Community for fear of being judged on my level of observance. And there was a lot to judge! When I finally got enough nerve one *Shabbat* to go to *shul* for the first time (with a hat to match my suit), it took everything I could muster to walk into the front doors of the building. I stood there for no more than a few minutes, feeling like a fish out of water, unable to breathe. I promptly turned around and walked home defeated. This scene repeated itself for months, until I finally got the courage to actually walk into the sanctuary. I felt like a fraud. I didn't know where to sit or what to do. I certainly didn't know which book to pick up or where they were in the service. On one of those brave walks to *shul* it looked like it would soon rain, so I decided to bring an umbrella. As I was walking, I passed a kind man whom I wished a "good *Shabbos*". He responded in kind and asked me if I was going to *shul*. I proudly told him "yes," thinking he was a visitor and needed directions. But he was gently trying to tell me that the umbrella was *muktzeh*, and not permitted to be carried on *Shabbat*. He didn't want me to be embarrassed by bringing the umbrella to *shul*. I thanked him and continued on my way until he was out of sight. Then I threw the umbrella into some nearby bushes and ran home, crying all the way.

Thankfully after some time in the Community, I made friends and started to learn what was going on around me. Once in a while, I would be on the right page of the *Siddur*, and if the *chazan* was slow and clear enough, I could even follow along while the Congregation was singing. It was those few moments of connecting with the *kehillah* that would keep me coming back. Those were powerful moments; to feel like I was part of the *davening* - part of the Jewish People, and that I could, in some small and incomplete way, do what every Jewish person should know how to do.

When Menashe and I were first married we used to "argue" about what type of school our children would attend. I wanted the best secular prep school and Menashe wanted a Jewish day school. As I spent more time in the Young Israel Community, I began to realize the importance of a Jewish education. I never wanted my kids to be in the situation that I found myself in - to be Jewish and to be completely ignorant about Judaism. Therefore, I finally agreed to enroll our first child Yael in pre-K at the local Jewish day school. The years flew by and soon my Yael began to know much more about our faith than I did, and her skills soon surpassed mine. After second grade, I could no longer help her with her Hebrew reading. Instead, she was soon helping me. Eventually when they were old enough to sit in *shul* with me, my daughters would help me find the right page. It was the beginning of something beautiful. I knew I was on the right path. More than that, I started to better understand and appreciate what had spurred my brother to so radically change his life.

School wasn't the only thing Menashe and I would argue about. A full description of our journey would be incomplete if I left out the extent to which Menashe was moving, growing and changing (everything!!!) at warp speed, while I was advancing at a snail's pace. Daily he would learn new *halachot* and *minhagim* (not to mention *chumrot*!) that he was so excited to add to our newly observant lives, which were already overflowing with change.

During Menashe's conversion process, we both grew to love, admire and respect Rabbi Davis (see [Dedication](#)), under whose auspices we would study. Over the year Menashe spent preparing for his conversion and learning with Rabbi Davis, we had a lot to cover and the Rabbi observed the dichotomy of our individual growth rates. He was very sensitive to my feelings of such dramatic change in our lives. Even more importantly, he was extremely sensitive to the impact our new lifestyle would have on my parents and my future (non-Jewish) mother-in-law, and how our transformation would affect those relationships. In deciding matters of *halachah*, he would often put great weight on our family's *shalom bayit*, and for this I will be eternally grateful. He also had the foresight and wisdom to occasionally tell Menashe to "chill out," and at other times to tell me to "get moving." With that guidance, we were able to gradually (and mostly) absorb the tremors that come with such dramatic change. After some time in the Community, our friends, family and Rabbi Davis collectively diagnosed Menashe to have an acute case of O.C.C.D. (Over-Compensating Convert Disorder). Menashe needed someone he completely respected to keep him in check. Because we both felt well-represented by Rabbi Davis and we both loved and respected him, we decided that we would make him <u>our</u> Rabbi, our *posek*. To this day, I often say that if it were not for Rabbi Davis, Menashe and I would not be married. Words cannot express how much we owe to Rabbi and his wife Meira for all they have given us.

When I have discussions with my friends who grew up in modern Orthodox homes, or even with my children, I often bring a different perspective. I tell them I will never know what it's like to look at being Jewish from their point of view. All I can do is look at it from my own life experiences. In hindsight, I could say, "ignorance is bliss." and life would be so much easier, SO MUCH EASIER, if we hadn't gone down this path. But it would also be devoid of meaning and moral guidance. Instead, my life is full of insight, self-reflection and a sense of freedom. The freedom that comes from knowing I have answers to the difficult questions and situations that come my way. I often try to find the meaning or message in the things that happen to or around me in this crazy world. I could have gone through life missing so many important and beautiful moments that I now know are truly from the Hand of *Hashem*. The challenge is to try to find G-d in everything. Occasionally, I look at the world around me and try to find significance in even the most mundane interactions or occurrences. Instead of "why is this happening to me," I often will find myself asking "what is the meaning behind what is happening?" To me this is the consequence of living a deliberate life, connected to *Hashem* and His *Torah*.

Menashe asked me to share my perspective of our Jewish journey in an <u>Introduction</u> to this book, which was compiled in honor of our son, Ayden Avraham, becoming a *Bar Mitzvah*. Ayden, our "number four," is such a special young man. He is tough and competitive, but he is also very sensitive and has the kindest heart. He is both passionate and compassionate, traits I pray he will carry with him throughout his life. Our family journey is ongoing, and each of our children, Ayden, Yael, Emma, and Benny, brings so much character and spark to our family unit. They are so special to us, unique in every way and truly exceptional in our eyes. We love you all so dearly.

Finally "אחרון אחרון חביב," "the very last is most beloved," (Rashi on Bereshit 33:2), I want to thank Menashe. Every relationship is a gamble. I was taking a calculated risk when I allowed you to look for a tiny hole in the brick wall I put up around me. You stole my heart with your humor, intelligence and stellar character (despite what I knew about you in college!). The only thing missing at the time was your religion. Ha! What a laugh we all have thinking back to those days in the beginning. But, I picked a winning lottery ticket. You have surpassed my expectations in everything. You are an adoring and understanding husband, committed to our marriage, which we are both always striving to make better and better with time. You're a devoted father and parent, with a strong will to do what is best, not necessarily what is easiest, for our children. You provide them with an honorable role model for a practicing "modern ultra-Orthodox Jew" in the very confusing world in which we live. You're a great friend, committed to your relationships, not just with me but those dearest to you as well. And to plagiarize from that famous *Torah* compiler, Menashe Frank, "We have both come so far, and we've done it together, with trust, and love and laughter and a few tears. For all of it, I simply say 'thank you.'"

J.C.F.
July 2017 / Av 5777

JAMIE'S FAMILY PHOTOS

Maternal great grandparents Sarah (Sarah Etyl) and Sam (Shalom) Canar

Sam and Sarah Canar; Maureen and Douglas Cohn; paternal great grandmothers Reva (Rikvah) Gerelick and Rose (Pesha) Cohn

Jamie's Family Photos — 13

Maternal grandparents Benjamin (Binyamin) and Gertrude (Gittle) Zevitz

Paternal grandparents Anne (Henya) and Bennett (Pinchas Leib) Cohn

The always talented
Annie Cohn

The Cohn Family's "Spanish Villa," 113 South 68th Avenue, Omaha, Nebraska

Maureen (Masha Chanah) Zevitz marries Douglas Brooks (Menachem Mendle HaKohain) Cohn

"Bootsie" and "Bootzie" Cohn

16 — אַךְ שָׂמֵחַ *Ach Sameach*

One of many honors bestowed on Maureen and Doug (now referred to as Bubbie and Zayde)

Levi and Shira Cohn and family, with the Cohns and Franks

BAT MITZVAH CERTIFICATE

Behold a good doctrine has been given you, forsake it not. (Prov 4:2)

בי לקח טוב נתתי לכם תורתי אל תעזבו

THIS IS TO RECORD THAT

פ׳גל לאה בת חיים מרדכי הלוי
HEBREW

Jamie Lynn Cohn
ENGLISH

CELEBRATED HER

בת מצוה

ON SABBATH ___ויקהל___

February 28 1981   I Adar 24 5741

IN THE PRESENCE OF CONGREGATION

Schaarai Zedek

Tampa, Florida
CITY

Rabbi Frank N. Sundheim
RABBI   SIGNATURE

Lillian G. Ohason
SIGNATURE

Bat Mitzvah certificate of Jamie (Faigel Leah) Cohn

YOM TOVIM

ROSH HASHANAH

5758

The Rambam says there are both "sleepers" and "dozers." The *shofar* wakes them both. The difference between them deals with mindset. The sleepers want to be asleep, while the dozers are praiseworthy, for they want to be awakened. The *pasuk* in *Tehillim* (89:16) states "Happy are those who know the *teruah* (the wail of the *shofar*)." Rav Moshe Feinstein states that "to know" means "to love." Those who know the *teruah* love the *shofar*, for it awakens them from their slumber in order to do *teshuvah*. These are the dozers the Rambam praises.

5759

MRF Note - In the month of *Elul* we prepare for the Days of Awe, *Rosh Hashanah* and *Yom Kippur*. Growing up in New Hampshire, I recall that there was a law that everyone inspect and fix his car every year in order to pass a state-mandated inspection. Problems that were left unaddressed during the year needed to be corrected in the pre-inspection period to ensure another year of operations. The same is true during *Elul*, the pre-inspection period of the soul.

5760

The Dubner Maggid – There once was a storekeeper who lost everything in a fire. He went to one of his main suppliers for help. The supplier promptly canceled a substantial debt that the storekeeper owed him, and gave him a line of credit through which to rebuild his business. When a friend of the storekeeper heard of what the supplier did for his friend, he promptly went to the supplier, whom he had never met, to request a loan for the same amount. The supplier refused the friend, explaining that he would only make such an arrangement with someone with whom he had done business. The supplier explained that he had made money in dealing with the storekeeper in the past and expected to again in the future. The arrangement was a good investment as to the storekeeper, yet the same could not be said about the friend. *Hashem*, the Ultimate Supplier, rewards regular attendance in *shul* in the same way. When we stand before Him on *Yom HaDin*, asking for a suitable arrangement for the coming year, it helps when he can quantify our "payments" to Him over the year just passed.

Some reasons for the *minhagim* of *Rosh Hashanah*:

1. Why do we use round *challah*? The *Gemara* tells us (a) it recalls the shape of the world, and on *Rosh Hashanah* the whole world is judged (Rosh Hashanah 16a); and (b) it recalls the shape of a *keter* and on *Rosh Hashanah* we crown *Hashem* as King of the Universe. (Rosh Hashanah 32a)

2. Why do we dip an apple in honey? When *Yitzchak* gave the blessings to *Yaacov* he said "the smell of my son is as the smell of a field that the Lord had blessed." (Bereshit 27:27) The *Gemara* (Taanit 28b) states that "field" there refers to an apple orchard. By dipping apples, we are asking *Hashem* for the blessing of *Yaacov* to be bestowed upon us, his descendants.

3. Why use honey? The *gematria* of davash is 306, which is the same as the expression "Av Harachamim," "Merciful Father." The Bnei Yissaschar explains that by dipping in the honey, we express confidence that *Hashem* will judge us as a father judges his child, with His Attribute of Mercy. (Maamar Chodesh Tishrei 2:13)

On *Rosh Hashanah* we are reminded of the story of righteous *Yael* killing the wicked *Sisra*. (Shoftim 4:21) The *Gemara* (Rosh Hashanah 33b) indicates that *Sisra's* evil mother cried 101 tears at the loss of her son. Sefer HaToda'ah explains that on *Rosh Hashanah* we blow the *shofar* 100 times to counter her tears of anger, but leave one tear which we recognize as from the purity of a mother's love for her son.

5761

Rav Avraham Pam – When engaging in the required introspection of *Elul* and *Tishrei*, one should not claim that because one learns some *Torah* and performs some *mitzvot* that he is righteous and has done enough to be considered Holy. *Hashem* tells us that "You shall be Holy, for I, *Hashem*, your G-d, am Holy." (Vayikra 19:2) The standard for the Jew is not to be as good as the slackers among us but to emulate *Hashem* himself.

Dr. Mark Jaffee – This year, the first day of *Rosh Hashanah* falls out on *Shabbat*. On *Shabbat* night we begin *Kiddush* with the *pasuk* that includes "Yom HaShishi..." "The Sixth Day...." (Bereshit 1:31) But yet we know that *Shabbat* is clearly the Seventh Day of the week. (Bereshit 2: 2,4) The simple explanation is that on the Sixth Day of Creation *Hashem* stopped creating and on the Seventh Day He "rested" (so to speak). But the *Gemara* (Shabbat 88a) states that "Yom HaShishi" is a reference not to the Sixth Day of Creation but to the Sixth Day of *Sivan*, which is *Shavuot*, the date of *Matan Torah*. It is only through our acceptance of the Torah that we come to perform the mitzvah of making *Kiddush* on *Shabbat*.

Tishrei is regarded as the Holiest month. It is the Seventh Month of the year, when counting from the first of *Nissan*, which is the beginning of the calendar for such calculations. (Rosh Hashanah 7a) In matters of time, the Seventh (e.g. *Shabbat, Shemittah, Omer*) is always sanctified.

Rabbi Edward Davis – The Jewish calendar is cyclical, not linear. Each year we come back to the time and conditions of each formative event in our history. The September 11th attacks in New York and Washington, D.C. occurred in the days preceding Creation, when the Universe was unstructured and void. Two days later, on *Rosh Hashanah, Hashem* began creating (recreating) and bringing order. Order for Jews is *Kedushah*. The *Pesach Seder* celebrates the freedom that accompanies order and contrasts the chaos that prevails in a state of slavery. The enemies of *Hashem* seek distance from Him by perpetuating the darkness that precedes order. Our job is to let the light of the *Torah* continue to bring about the perfection of *Hashem's* Creation, which is celebrated on *Rosh Hashanah*.

Rabbi Asher Resnick – The *Mussaf* service of *Rosh Hashanah* addresses the three major theological mistakes that people often make: (1) that there is no G-d, for which *Malchiut* declares that *Hashem* exists and we crown

Him as King; (2) that while there is a G-d, He has no connection to the World, for which *Zichronot* declares that He is engaged in His Creation; and (3) that while G-d exists and is involved in the world, He has no special connection to the Jewish People, for which we recite *Shofrot* which declares that He gave us His *Torah* at *Har Sinai* and made us His Special Nation.

5762

The *Gemara* (Rosh Hashanah 11a) tells us that Rabbi Eliezer states that *Avraham*, *Yitzchak* and *Yaacov* were all born in the month of *Tishrei*, which is therefore referred to as "Yerach HaEisanim," "the month of the strong."

5763

Rabbi Yossi Jankovits – The Admor of Gur points out that hope springs eternal in the heart of every Jew. This is evident in the fact that at *Minchah* on *Erev Rosh Hashanah* we still ask *Hashem* to "Baraich HaShanah HaZot," "to Bless this year." Despite the fact that there are literally only minutes left in the current year, the Jew still expects *Hashem's* Blessings and Bounty.

5764

Rabbi Yossi Jankovits – The Divrei Yoel, quoting the Yismach Moshe, questions whether *Akeidat Yitzchak*, which we recite as the *Torah* reading of the Second Day of *Rosh Hashanah* (Bereshit 22:1-19), was really such a test for *Avraham Avinu*, since *Hashem* Himself directed that he do it. He concludes that *Hashem* actually removed some of *Avraham's* clarity in order to test him, which is evidenced by the verse "vayar et HaMakom mairachok," "and he perceived *HaMakom* from afar." (Bereshit 22:4) "HaMakom," literally "the Place," could be a reference to the site of the *Akeidah* (i.e., *Har Moriah*) or to *Hashem* Himself (the "Place" in which all else exists). The latter reading would indicate that *Hashem* concealed Himself from *Avraham*, requiring him to struggle to believe in the authenticity of the Divine Imperative he had previously received. It is precisely this struggle, which he clearly overcame, that gave the Jews our extraordinary spiritual strength that we have drawn upon over the centuries that followed, and what we invoke as a *zechut* for ourselves on *Rosh Hashanah*.

Rabbi Yossi Jankovits – The *pasuk* declares "Tzedek, tzedek tirdof...," "Righteousness, righteousness you shall pursue...," (Devarim 16:20), meaning that one should be a *tzaddik* in stages, not all at once. This is the message of *Elul*: that all meaningful change is lasting only if undertaken incrementally. The *Shofar*, the representative symbol of *Elul*, is blown from the small end with sound emerging from the wider end. To blow it the opposite way is *assur* according to *halachah*. (Rosh Hashanah 27b) The lesson is that little changes bring big results. We see this philosophy in *Yaacov Avinu*, when he rejects his brother *Eisav's* offer to "travel together." *Yaacov* tells *Eisav* "v'ani etnahalah l'iti l'regel...," "I will make my way at a slow pace...." (Bereshit 33:14). The *rashei teivot* of his words are "vav," "aleph," "lamed," and "lamed." Unscrambled, that spells "אלול," "Elul!"

5765

Rabbi Yissocher Frand – In the pre-holiday *selichot* that we recite in the early morning in the days leading up to and including the *Yamim Noraim*, we declare to *Hashem* that "we come like paupers before you." Rav Avraham Pam points out that this declaration is not what it appears to be. Most would think that we are merely imploring *Hashem* for mercy and sustenance as a beggar does to someone of means. Few would take such a declaration literally, since most are confident with their financial status as they enter *Rosh Hashanah*. Yet Rav Pam states that this declaration is to be taken literally - that since one's entire year, including his level of income, health, and entire life's situation, is decided on *Rosh Hashanah*, the *Yom HaDin*, one is, in a very real sense, standing before *Hashem* as a pauper. The account is, so to speak, set back to zero, and *Hashem* makes a new calculation as to what will be allowed to each of us in the coming year. Yet nearly each one of us fails to appreciate this. We enter *Yom HaDin* with money in the bank, a portfolio of stock perhaps, a house, car, and, hopefully, good health. We don't truly expect that any of those things are going to be taken away from us in the process. They are locked away, guaranteed and secured. Yet we can look at the effects of the Expulsion of Jews from *Gush Katif* and the ravages of Hurricane Katrina in the Gulf area as proof of the futility of such an outlook. Of course *Hashem* can, G-d forbid, take it all away in a blink of an eye. If we appreciated the reality which we face on *Rosh Hashanah*, we would approach *Hashem* in fearful reverence, intent upon securing a good decree based upon sincere entreaties that recognize Him as the Source of all we have.

Rabbi Edward Davis – *Rosh Hashanah* is about *teshuvah*. The *Gemara* (Berachot 34b) states that in the place where a *baal teshuvah* stands a *tzaddik gamor* cannot. This expression may simply refer to the notion that a *baal teshuvah*, by accepting the *Torah*, literally stands again at *Har Sinai*, where his *neshamah* originally made the same acceptance, while a *frum* Jew who is not committed to renewal of his connection to the *Torah* is simply not standing in the same place – *Har Sinai*.

5766

Rabbi Yossi Jankovits – There is an opinion, based on Likutei Moharan, that the reason for the *minhag* not to sleep during the day of *Rosh Hashanah* is that it was on that day that *Adam HaRishon* was formed, sinned and consequently brought death to the world. The Gemara (Berachot 57b) teaches that sleep is considered $1/60^{th}$ of death, and we therefore avoid it as a *tikkun* for *Adam's* error.

5769

Reb Josh Levine – The Baal Shem Tov points out that the *U'Netana Tokef* prayer of *Rosh Hashanah* states that *Hashem* "remembers what is forgotten." This can be either a positive or negative for a Jew, depending on his approach to the Holy Day. If one forgets his *aveirot* and fails to face up to them, *Hashem* will "remember" them and hold him accountable. Conversely, if one forgets the *mitzvot* he did and refrains from invoking them for *Hashem's* favorable Consideration in His Judgment, then *Hashem* will Himself "remember" them as a merit.

5770

Rabbi Edward Davis — In the story of the *Akeidah*, read on the Second Day of *Rosh Hashanah*, the *Torah* indicates that, following the unfathomable religious experience of *Yitzchak* and *Avraham* on *Har Moriah*, they returned to *Eliezer* and *Yishmael*. (Rashi on Bereshit 22:3) There the *Torah* specifically states "vayakoomu, vayail'chu yachdav . . . ," "they [all] arose and went [back] together . . . ." (Bereshit 22:19) This indicates a remarkable humility on the part of *Yitzchak* and *Avraham* where, despite their superior spiritual achievement, neither flaunted a "Holier than Thou" attitude towards *Eliezer* and *Yishmael*. This is a model for all Orthodox Jews in how to relate to their less-religious Brethren. Significantly, however, in preparing to proceed with *Yitzchak* towards the transcendent *Akeidah* event in service to *Hashem*, Avraham insisted that *Eliezer* and *Yishmael* "shivu l'chem po, im hachamor," "remain here by yourselves with the donkey." (Bereshit 22:5) They clearly were not to be included in this spiritual occasion meant only for the progenitors of the Jewish People, and Rav Joseph B. Soloveitchik always compared *Eliezer* and *Yishmael* in this setting to Reform and Conservative leaders. Perhaps, therefore, the combined lessons of the *Akeidah* are that one should distance oneself from unworthy influences when seeking personal spiritual growth, but upon achievement of such growth, one must not denigrate those unworthy influences, but rather remain in contact for the purpose of modeling proper religious behavior.

5771

Chasam Sofer — Parashat Nitzavim, which is read annually around the time of *Rosh Hashanah*, begins "אַתֶּם נִצָּבִים הַיּוֹם כֻּלְּכֶם לִפְנֵי ה' אלקיכם רָאשֵׁיכֶם שִׁבְטֵיכֶם זִקְנֵיכֶם וְשֹׁטְרֵיכֶם כֹּל אִישׁ יִשְׂרָאֵל," "You are all standing this day before Hashem, your G-d, the leaders of your tribes, your elders and your officers, every man of Israel." (Devarim 29:9) This is a reference to standing together before the King of kings on *Rosh Hashanah,* and the "all" is meant to include not only those physically present but those spiritually present as well. On *Rosh Hashanah* the souls of one's deceased relatives stand beside him and pray on his behalf. This explains why we do not recite *Hallel* on this *Yom Tov* when we would otherwise want to add additional praises to *Hashem.* The *pasuk* clearly tells us that "לֹא הַמֵּתִים יְהַלְלוּ קָהּ וְלֹא כָּל יֹרְדֵי דוּמָה", "The dead will not praise G-d, nor all those who descend to the grave" (Tehillim 115:17). Because the dead are present and unable to join us, the living refrain from praising *Hashem* through *Hallel.*

5772

Rabbi Yosef Weinstock — *Akeidat Yitzchak* is the *Torah* portion read on the Second Day of *Rosh Hashanah.* The final *aliyah,* which follows the overwhelming test of the *Akeidah,* may demonstrate an additional test of *Avraham.* Specifically, *Avraham,* in being told of the recent births of many children to his brother *Nachor* (Bereshit 22:20-24), realizes that the world at large has gone on merrily without noticing the pain and struggle that he has endured. As humans, it hurts us to realize that even while we are dealing with a major life issue the rest of the world is generally oblivious to it. The realization presented a challenge to *Avraham* that could have manifested in the form of anger, depression or regret, but *Avraham's emunah* held firm in the understanding that he and his son had sanctified *Hashem's* Name. MRF Note — This calls to mind an occasion following the birth of my first child. I entered the hospital elevator with two dozen red roses for my wife. My pride and elation must have been apparent, and the middle-aged couple in the elevator asked if I had recently had a baby. I answered in the affirmative and reflectively asked if they were at the hospital for the same reason. They sadly indicated that they had just arrived from out of town because their adult daughter had been in a serious car accident overnight. Their response abruptly reminded me that most people visiting a hospital are not there for a happy reason, something I had entirely ignored in my personal euphoric situation. Perhaps the *mussar* lesson in the story of *Avraham* and *Nachor* is that during times of personal good fortune each of us should at least be sensitive to the fact that there are others around us that are residing on the other end of the emotion spectrum.

Rabbi Ephraim Wachsman – There are two *Rosh Hashanah* holidays that Jews observe: the first of *Tishrei* and the first of *Nissan*. When counting from the first day of *Nissan*, there are six full months representing the six days that precede the *Shabbat*: *Nissan*, *Iyar*, *Sivan*, *Tammuz*, *Av* and *Elul*. *Tishrei*, then, is the seventh month, equivalent to *Shabbat*, and therefore *Elul* is the equivalent of *Erev Shabbat*. One's "Shabbat" (i.e. *Tishrei*, with all its holidays) will only be as successful as his "*Erev Shabbat*" in *Elul*. Proper preparation makes for a meaningful holiday season.

5773

Rabbi Eli Mansour – In the first *berachah* of the *Shemoneh Esrei*, *Hashem* is referred to as "Melech, Ozer u'Moshiah u'Magen," "King, Helper, and Savior and Shield." This is a reference to the progression of the *Yom Tov* Season: "Melech" refers to *Rosh Hashanah* when *Hashem* is crowned King of the World; "Ozer" refers to *Hashem* as our Help in repenting during the *Aseret Yemei Teshuvah*; "Moshiah" refers to *Hashem* saving us from sin (and therefore death) on *Yom Kippur*; and "Magen" refers to the protection of the *sukkah* on *Sukkot*.

YOM KIPPUR

5757

On *Yom Kippur* we dress in white to indicate that we are like angels, without sin. Like angels, we have no need for food or drink, or, in theory, to sit down during the lengthy davening. (Yalkut Shimoni remez 578)

5758

On *Yom Kippur* we are commanded to engage in the painful work of *teshuvah*: to honestly look within ourselves, regret our failings, and resolve to do better. The task is daunting. During the *Minchah* service we read the *Haftarah* of *Yonah*, which provides inspiration as an example where man feels he is not up to the challenge that *Hashem* gives him, yet *Hashem* dictates and proves otherwise.

5759

Regarding the first day of Creation, the *Torah* states "... וַיְהִי עֶרֶב וַיְהִי בֹקֶר יוֹם אֶחָד," "... and it was evening and morning, Day One." (Bereshit 1:5) The other days of Creation are referred to in an ordinal way: "Second Day" or "Third Day," but Day One is not referred to as "First Day." The *Midrash* (Yalkut Shemoni remez 4) says this is a reference to *Yom Kippur*. Because no other beings had yet been created, it was the Day of The One, *Hashem*. With the creation of the angels on the Second Day (Midrash Rabbah, Bereshit 1:3) the illusion was created of existence apart from *Hashem*. In the Days of *Mashiach* we will return to the universal understanding and absolute clarity as to the Oneness of *Hashem*. *Yom Kippur* is a glimpse into this Oneness that was manifested on Day One. In fact, the *Talmud* (Yoma 20a) states that the *gematria* of "השטן," "the satan," is 364, indicating that for 364 days of the year the *satan* creates destructive illusions to distract us from properly contemplating *Hashem*. Yet on one day, Day One, which is *Yom Kippur*, we can overcome the illusions and connect in an awe-inspiring and meaningful way.

In the *Yom Kippur* service, the *Kohain Gadol* would change clothes and enter the *mikvah* both before going into the *Kodesh HaKadoshim* (Vayikra

16:4) and afterwards. (Vayikra 16:28) Surely, going from a less Holy/pure environment to a more Holy/pure environment would dictate changing and dunking before entering the Holy of Holies, but why would the opposite require changing and dunking as well? Perhaps because retaining *Kedushah* is harder than preparing for it, and people require extra effort and assistance to "hold on" to closeness to *Hashem*. This is certainly a lesson we can apply in making *Havdalah*, which is our attempt to hold on to the sanctity of *Shabbat* and *Yom Tov*.

5760

Baal Shem Tov – A central theme of *Yom Kippur* is forgiveness. To be forgiven by *Hashem* we must forgive others. The *Gemara* (Rosh Hashanah 17b) relates that "אמר לו כל זמן שישראל חוטאין יעשו לפני כסדר הזה ואני מוחל להם," "[Hashem] said to [Moshe] whenever Yisrael sins let Them do before me this order [of prayer]." *Hashem* could have instructed *Moshe* that the Jews should say the required prayers when they are seeking forgiveness for their sins, yet He instructs them to do the prayers, meaning take action to forgive others, in order to thereby gain their own atonement.

5761

Beginning on *Rosh Hashanah* and culminating on *Yom Kippur* we engage in an intensive *teshuvah* process. The *Mishnah* (Avot 2:15) states "רַבִּי אֱלִיעֶזֶר אוֹמֵר וְשׁוּב יוֹם אֶחָד לִפְנֵי מִיתָתְךָ," "Rabbi Eliezer says . . . repent one day before your death." The *Gemara* (Shabbat 153a) records that his students asked him the obvious question: does one know what day he is to die?" Rabbi Eliezer responded that because the date of death is unknown, and because *teshuvah* is required even up to the date of death, one must be engaged in the *teshuvah* process constantly through his entire life, not merely, for example, on *Yom Kippur*.

Rabbi Yisroel Ciner – The *Gemara* (Rosh Hashanah 17a) states "רבא אמר כל המעביר על מדותיו מעבירין לו על כל פשעיו שנאמר נושא עון ועובר על פשע

למי נושא עון למי שעובר על פשע," "Rava said whoever passes over his claims [about others], all his transgressions are passed over [by Hashem], as it is said '[Hashem] bears sins and passes over transgressions.' Whose sins does He bear? The one who passes on the transgressions [of others]." This concept can be demonstrated in the example of someone who possesses the *middah* of anger, yet he "passes over" his natural inclination to berate another person by controlling his anger. In such a case *Hashem* will overlook his sins as a reward, demonstrating the attribute of *middah keneged middah*. The *Chofetz Chaim* points out that in the *Avinu Malkeinu* prayer we beseech *Hashem* to write us in the Book of Merits. In doing so we are impliedly asking Him not to scrutinize too closely the *mitzvot* we accomplished during the year, for they certainly contain blemishes which diminish their value. Instead, we implore him to "pass by" those blemishes without applying scrutiny, giving each of us the benefit of the doubt just as we have hopefully done to others. By accepting our fellow Jews at face value, we can expect *Hashem* to do the same for us.

5762

Rabbi Leib Kelemen – The *Yom Kippur davening* invokes the *Torah's* description of an enigmatic service involving two goats. (Vayikra 16:7-11, 20-22) Specifically, one goat is sacrificed by the *Kohain Gadol* "to *Hashem*," while "וְהַשָּׂעִיר אֲשֶׁר עָלָה עָלָיו הַגּוֹרָל לַעֲזָאזֵל יָעֳמַד חַי לִפְנֵי ה' לְכַפֵּר עָלָיו לְשַׁלַּח אֹתוֹ לַעֲזָאזֵל הַמִּדְבָּרָה," "And the he-goat upon which the lot 'For Azazael' came up, shall be placed alive before Hashem to atone upon it, and to send it away to Azazael, into the desert." (Vayikra 16:10) Jewish sensibilities are startled by a command, even from the *Torah*, to send an animal "to Azazael," for it appears to be directing *Bnei Yisrael* to commit *avodah zareh*. The goat that is sent to *Azazael* is not, however, a *korban*, for an animal is made a *korban* only through *shechitah*, and the *Gemara* makes clear this goat is directed to be thrown from a cliff. (Yoma 67a) So while the ceremony is clearly not *avodah zareh*, what does it accomplish? Imagine a king who commands his royal chef to prepare and send a wonderful and extravagant dinner to a lowly palace guard. In fulfilling the king's directive, the chef does so not out of love for the guard but rather for the purpose of honoring the king. Yet by providing the scrumptious meal, the chef, despite his intention, does engender favor in the eyes of the palace guard, which is what the king truly desires. *Azazael* is the spirit of *Eisav*, the *yetzer hara*, the Accuser, who is intent on harming *Bnei Yisrael*. *Hashem*, our King, directs us to placate *Azazael* on *Yom Kippur* in a number of ways. In the times of the Temple we had the "scapegoat" ceremony, and today we are commanded to eat heartily before *Yom Kippur*.

5763

Rabbi Yossi Jankovits – The *pasuk* states "שֵׁשֶׁת יָמִים תֵּעָשֶׂה מְלָאכָה וּבַיּוֹם הַשְּׁבִיעִי שַׁבַּת שַׁבָּתוֹן מִקְרָא קֹדֶשׁ כָּל מְלָאכָה לֹא תַעֲשׂוּ שַׁבָּת הִוא לַה' בְּכֹל מוֹשְׁבֹתֵיכֶם," "For six days, work may be performed, but on the seventh day, it is a complete rest day, a Holy convocation; you shall not perform any work. It is a Shabbat to Hashem in all your dwelling places." (Vayikra 23:3) While this would seem to be a straightforward reference to the six workdays and *Shabbat*, the Vilna Gaon interprets the "six days" as the two (first and last) days of *Pesach*, one day of *Shavuot*, one day of *Rosh Hashanah* and two (first and last) days of *Sukkot*, when "work can be performed," meaning we may cook and carry for the benefit of the day. The "seventh day" mentioned in the *pasuk* is *Yom Kippur*, "Shabbat Shabbaton," a "complete rest day," when even cooking and carrying is prohibited, as is the case with *Shabbat*.

Rabbi Yosef Kalatsky – *Yom Kippur* marks the end of *Aseret Yemei Teshuvah*, and our Sages instruct us that humility is a prerequisite to *teshuvah*. The *Midrash* Yalkut Shimoni (remez 752) tells us that, prior to their "final showdown," *Moshe* went to *Korach's* tent to try to work things out. The sons of *Korach* "covered their faces with the ground," when *Moshe* entered their home, which indicates that they were embarrassed to face him. They were in a quandary because *halachah* dictated that they should rise in respect for their *Rebbe*, but they knew he was their father's rival. This predicament embarrassed them yet they ultimately stood up. In doing so, they had the stirrings of *teshuvah*, which they eventually embraced, saving them from the death that their father suffered. This aspect of shame/conscience is a critical to the *teshuvah* process.

5764

Rabbi Moshe Peretz Gilden – On *Yom Kippur* we seek to seal a favorable Judgment from *Hashem*. The *Gemara* (Shabbat 127b) states "ת"ר הדן חבירו לכף זכות דנין אותו לזכות," "Our Sages say that one who gives his friend that benefit of the doubt is given the benefit of the doubt [by Hashem]." Yet one could ask an obvious question: Does *Hashem* possess any "doubt" such that He should judge favorably as a result? Rabbi Yissocher Frand answers with an analogy. On *Yom Kippur* we are all like students, providing incomplete and incorrect exam answers to our Teacher, *Hashem*. If we act leniently in judging our fellow "students," this causes *Hashem*, so to speak, to act towards us like a teacher who is an "easy grader," looking for something of value even in a student's incorrect answer. Yet failing to give our fellow students the benefit of the doubt causes *Hashem* to act as a "tough grader," disregarding the entirety of our incorrect answers.

5765

Rabbi Edward Davis – On *Yom Kippur* we focus on personal *teshuvah*. The *Gemara* (Berachot 34b; Sanhedrin 99a) states "מקום שבעלי תשובה עומדין צדיקים גמורים אינם עומדין," "In the place where *baalei teshuvah* stand total tzaddikim cannot stand." The simple understanding is that in (re)accepting the *Torah*, a *baal teshuvah* is, in some metaphysical way, standing at *Har Sinai*, where historically, every person present experienced a Divine Revelation unmatched in history. (Devarim 4:11, 12) By reconnecting to *Torah* the *baal teshuvah* is reexperiencing *Har Sinai*, something the consistently observant Jew is unable to do.

5766

The *Talmud* (Berachot 34b; Sanhedrin 99a) indicates that in the place a *baal teshuvah* stands a total *tzaddik* cannot. Perhaps there is an analogy to be drawn with the struggle for weight loss. A person who has been greatly overweight feels exhilaration in losing a few pounds through dieting or exercise. Although he may still be overweight, he celebrates his accomplishments and is inspired to continue improvement. The lifelong fitness adherent, however, would be aghast to be at even the reduced weight of the dieter, since he has never been more than a pound or two over his ideal weight. So it is also with the *tzaddik*, who never fell to a level of spiritual debasement, where the incremental journey back is a series of exhilarating victories.

5767

Rabbi Yossi Jankovits – With respect to the incident of the *cheit haeigel*, described in Parashat Ki Tisa, the *Torah* text is silent on the question as to whether *Shevet Levy* participated in the sin or even stood by in silence as it took place. And yet, the *pasuk* tells us that after the sin, "וַיַּעֲמֹד מֹשֶׁה בְּשַׁעַר הַמַּחֲנֶה וַיֹּאמֶר מִי לַה' אֵלָי וַיֵּאָסְפוּ אֵלָיו כָּל בְּנֵי לֵוִי," "Moshe stood in the gate of the camp and said: 'Whoever is for Hashem, [come] to me!' And all the sons of Levy gathered around him." (Shemot 32:26) More than merely joining *Moshe*, we are told the Tribe of *Levy* took up arms to kill their offending brethren. (Shemot 32:28) Perhaps the lesson is that when their *Rebbe* pointed out the seriousness of the situation and demanded immediate *teshuvah*, they responded and made the right choice. The same could be said about the Jews in the *Chanukah* story (where, incidentally, the identical language "מִי לַה' אֵלָי," was stated). The point was that even where the members of *Bnei Yisrael* might have engaged in prohibited acts of assimilation up to that point, at the moment their *Rebbe* demanded *teshuvah*, some responded and were saved, and many others were slaughtered in a civil war. The message has particular applicability to the *avodah* of *Yom Kippur*. When we are made aware of our sinful acts by the wise persons around us, we must take heed and save ourselves from the penalties associated with sinning and failing to listen to the Sages.

Rabbi Yossi Jankovits – Rabbi Jankovits's grandfather (Reb Menachem Mendel, a'h) was a *shochet* in Romania after World War II. At that time, it was illegal to slaughter meat without the permission of the Communist authorities due to scarcity. When it was almost *Yom Tov*, he *shechted* a cow and his son (Reb Yisroel, a'h, Rabbi Jankovits's father) went to deliver the meat to the local Jewish community. Reb Yisroel was caught by the authorities and his trial was scheduled for *Yom Kippur*. Reb Menachem Mendel went to the Damesek Eliezer for advice. The *Rebbe* quoted a *pasuk* from Parashat Mikeitz. In response to *Yehudah's* plea to *Yaacov* to allow the Brothers to take *Binyamin* to *Mitzrayim*, *Yaacov* says "וְקֵל שַׁקַּי יִתֵּן לָכֶם רַחֲמִים לִפְנֵי הָאִישׁ וְשִׁלַּח לָכֶם אֶת אֲחִיכֶם אַחֵר וְאֶת בִּנְיָמִין," "And may the Al-mighty G-d grant you compassion before the man, and he will release to you your other brother and Binyamin, . . ." (Bereshit 43:14) Aside from the clear thematic connection, the *rashei teivot* of the beginning of the *pasuk* (disregarding the connector "vav") are "aleph," "shin," "yud," "lamed," and "raish," which are the letters that comprise "יִשְׂרָאֵל," the name of the accused! The *Rebbe* assured Reb Menachem Mendel that his son would prevail and on *Yom Kippur* the case was dropped. This story is brought down in a *sefer* about the Damesek Eliezer, and Rabbi Jankovits confirmed this story with his father in his last days.

5768

Reb Ephraim Sobol – On *Yom Kippur* we read about the "Asarah Harugei Malkut," "The Ten Martyrs" who, we are told, were murdered as atonement for the Sale of *Yosef*. According to the *Midrash* (Pirkei D'Rabbi Eliezer 37 and Targum Yonatan, based on Amos), many of the five prohibitions of *Yom Kippur* can be connected to the Sale. The Brothers bought shoes with the twenty pieces of silver (Pirkei d'Rabbi Eliezer 38) and wearing shoes is prohibited; they sold *Yosef* to *Mitzrayim*, the epitome of sexual immorality, as demonstrated by *Potiphar's* wife (Bereshit 39:7-12) and marital relations are prohibited; the pit into which they threw *Yosef* had no water in it (Bereshit 37:24) and washing is prohibited; and after selling *Yosef*, the Brothers sat down to a meal (Bereshit 37:25) and eating is prohibited. MRF Note: The *Midrash* does not provide a clear connection between the *Yom Kippur* prohibition of anointing with oil and the Sale of *Yosef*, but it is interesting that immediately following the Sale, the narrative of the *Torah* is interrupted by the seemingly unrelated story of *Yehudah* and *Tamar* (Bereshit 38:1-30), which our Sages struggle to explain. The Midrash Rabbah (Bereshit 85) points out that *Tamar's* firstborn child was *Peretz*, who was a progenitor of *David HaMelech* (Rut 4:18-22), who is the progenitor of *Mashiach*. *Mashiach*, spelled "משיח," comes from the Hebrew root "משח," which means to anoint, for every Jewish king past and future must be anointed with oil to serve.

5770

Rabbi Yissocher Frand – At the end of each *Shemoneh Esrei* of the *Yom Kippur* davening, there is a puzzling *pasuk* that reads "אלוקי, עד שלא נוצרתי איני כדאי ועכשיו שנוצרתי, כאילו לא נוצרתי," "My G-d, before I was formed I was unworthy, and now that I am formed, it is as if I had not been formed." *Chazal* read this to mean as follows: before a person is brought by *Hashem* into the world, there is a recognition by his *neshamah* that he is destined to live in a certain time, in a certain place, under certain conditions, and is expected to have a positive effect and to make an impact in fulfilling his life mission. The *neshamah* feels unworthy to the challenge, yet *Hashem* deems it necessary to form the person and bring him into the world for his particular purpose. The greatest disappointment comes with the realization that it is "as if" one has never been formed, for he has utterly failed to merit the gifts and powers bestowed upon him by *Hashem* in failing to achieve his purpose.

5771

Rabbi Mordechai Becher – When reciting the *Shema*, we do not recite aloud "baruch Shem Kavod Malchuto l'olam va'ed," "Blessed is the Name of His Honored Kingship forever," except on *Yom Kippur*, when we are compared to angels. (Yalkut Shemoni remez 578) But why do we say it out loud for *Maariv* after *Kol Nidre* rather than at *Maariv* after *Neilah*? Are we not closer in emulating the attributes of *malachim* after a day of prayer and fasting, rather than merely one hour after eating? The proof is brought from the episode of *Yaacov* and his ladder, where the angels are famously moving up and down, rather than down (from Heaven) and then up. (Bereshit 28:12) *Chazal* famously indicate there that the angels dedicated to accompany *Yaacov* outside of *Eretz Yisrael* were descending for that purpose (apparently the angels escorting him within Israel could not leave the Land for that purpose). But commentators note that this took place on *Har Moriah*, where *Yaacov* was still separated by both time and geography from physically departing from the Land. (Rashi on Bereshit 28:11) The differentiator was direction or "vector." *Yaacov* was headed *chutz l'Aretz*, even while he was in the *Aretz*, and for that reason he needed "exile angels" to escort him even while he was still in the Land. The same applies to our approach to *Yom Kippur*. After *Kol Nidre* we are directed towards Holiness; afterwards, despite having been cleansed in the process, we are on a vector towards physicality. It's not necessarily where one is, but rather where one is going. MRF Note – The same can be used to distinguish the fate of *Yishmael* in the *midbar* (Rashi on Bereshit 21:17) in Parashat Vayeira from the fate of the *ben sorer u'moreh* (Devarim 21:21) in Parashat Ki Teitzei. As Rabbi Eli Mansour teaches, *Hashem* spared *Yishmael* because he was engaged in *teshuvah* at the time of his judgment, while the rebellious son, despite having not yet sinned enough to warrant death, was clearly on a negative trajectory and therefore was killed.

5772

Reb Michael Baratz – Rabbi Yisroel Salanter once asked the owner of an upscale coffee shop in Vilna why he charged a full ruble for a cup of coffee that cost him only 25 kopeks to make. The proprietor replied that the price included not merely the coffee but the ambience of the shop as well. He pointed to the beautiful serving dishes, the art that adorned the walls, the soothing music provided by a violinist and a courteous and professional wait staff that attended to the customer's every need. It was the totality of the experience, explained the owner, that warranted such an exorbitant price. At this, Rav Salanter became ecstatic, thanking the owner profusely, for he had answered for him a nagging question: why does a simple glass of water merit the *berachah* of *shehakol*? In fact, reasoned the *Rav*, we are "paying" *Hashem* for the totality of the innumerable gifts he bestows upon us in drinking the water. We grasp and hold the glass with our hand, we see the clear liquid with clear eyes, we drink it in a house, surrounded by loved ones, we are able to pass the water in the proper time, and so on. It is this *kavanah* we should try to achieve when making *berachot*, which will, in turn, imbue us with a sense of *hakarat hatov* for the myriad blessings we enjoy.

5773

Rabbi Yaakov Weinberg – The well-known *Mishnah* is sometimes poorly translated: "אֵיזֶהוּ עָשִׁיר, הַשָּׂמֵחַ בְּחֶלְקוֹ," does not mean "Who is a rich man? He who is <u>satisfied</u> with his portion," but rather "He who is <u>happy</u> with his portion." The implication is that one need not be satisfied with his lot and can legitimately aspire for a greater portion, especially in *ruchniut*. He must be happy, however, regarding each level he achieves in his journey upward. Reb Abie Moses reads the *Mishnah* differently. Who is a rich man? "הַשָּׂמֵחַ בְּחֶלְקוֹ," The one who is happy in <u>his</u> [friend's] portion!" Combined, this wisdom brings a powerful message: be happy, but not necessarily satisfied, with what you have achieved, and certainly be happy, and not jealous, with what others have achieved.

SUKKOT

5757

The *Arba'ah Minim* that are taken on *Sukkot* are sometimes compared to the key physical components of man. The Chinuch (Mitzvah 324) instructs us that the *etrog* is compared to the heart; the *lulav* is compared to the spine; the *hadassim* are compared to the eyes; and the *aravot* are compared to the lips. In the same way that we take all *Arba'ah Minim* together in service of *Hashem*, so too must the Jew sanctify his entire body in service to his Creator.

5758

One of the *Arba'ah Minim* that *Bnei Yisrael* are commanded to take on *Sukkot* is "arvay nachal," "brook willows." (Vayikra 23:40) The root is "ערב," which is identical to the Hebrew word for guarantor. Every Jew is the guarantor of the safety and wellbeing of every other Jew, which is manifested in our adherence to *Torah*. On *Har Sinai*, *Bnei Yisrael* famously said "naaseh v'nishma," "<u>we</u> will do and <u>we</u> will hear." (Shemot 24:7) That "we" is used with respect to accepting the *Torah* is evidence that we were accepting for the Community as a whole and guaranteeing the future performance of *mitzvot* of all our fellow Jews.

5759

The *sukkah* commemorates the Clouds of Glory that protected *Bnei Yisrael* in the *midbar*. (Sukkah 11b) The *halachah* indicates that a *sukkah* with three sides is kosher, yet the *Anaini HaKavod* surrounded the Jews on all sides. This may be an indication that in the *midbar* the Jews were sustained by *Hashem* and had no need to work or otherwise engage in the material world. We, however, must do so, and we therefore leave open one side of the *sukkah* as a reminder of this reality.

Aruch LaNer – The *Gemara* (Sukkah 2a, 2b) outlines the difference of opinion among *Rabbah*, *Rabbi Zeira* and *Rava* as to why the *Mishnah* dictates that a *sukkah* cannot have walls higher than twenty *amot*, about thirty-five feet. *Rabbah* states that the eye normally does not travel that high, so a person sitting in such a *sukkah* does not have the feeling of being enclosed by the *s'chach* roof. *Rabbi Zeira* indicates that the *s'chach* of the *sukkah* must provide shade and in the case of a very high *sukkah*, the walls, and not the s'chach, would provide the shade. Finally, *Rava* opines that a *sukkah* with such a high roof would be regarded as permanent, not temporary, which is a *halachic* requirement. These three views represent the Three Pillars of Righteousness: *Rabbah* invokes Fear of *Hashem*; *Rabbi Zeira* invokes Trust in *Hashem*; and *Rava* invokes Humility. To fear *Hashem*, I need to perceive Him before me, just as one must be able to perceive the *s'chach* of a *sukkah*. To trust *Hashem* I must feel as if my protection comes from Him, just as one must obtain shade from the *s'chach* of the *sukkah*. Finally, to remain humble I must see this world as temporary, like a kosher *sukkah*.

5760

Each of the *Arba'ah Minim* has a unique aspect of taste and smell, which the *Midrash* (Vayikra Rabbah 30:12) uses as a comparison to different kinds of Jews. Taste refers to *Torah* knowledge, which is a measurable quality, and smell alludes to *mitzvah* merits, which is more difficult to quantify. The *etrog* has both taste and smell, and describes a Jew of erudition and high character. The *lulav* has a taste but no smell, describing one who excels in learning but not as much in *middot*. The *hadassim* have a smell but no taste, alluding to the Jew of high moral substance but without *Torah* learning. And finally the *aravot* have neither taste nor smell, describing an *am haaretz*. What is unique about the *Arba'ah Minim* is that individually they are worthless on *Sukkot*. One must have all four species together to fulfill the *mitzvah*. The Midrash Rabbah instructs that in the same way, while Jews may vary in learning and observance, they must be united to be effective.

Rabbi Yaacov Asher Sinclair - Ironically, while the *aravot* are commonly regarded as the least of the *Arba'ah Minim*, the *Gemara* (Sukkah 45a) points out that only the *aravot* have independent significance as demonstrated on *Hoshana Rabbah*. This may be based on the fact that *aravot* are sometimes compared to the lips of man, indicating that at the very least *Hashem* desires our prayers, which is accomplished with the lips. Alternatively, the *aravot* are compared to Jews not possessing *Torah* and *mitzvot*, and we know that *Hashem* takes pleasure in and seeks connection with the least of His Children.

Tur Shulchan Aruch (Orach Chayim 417) states that the *Shalosh Regalim* correspond to the Three *Avot*. *Yaacov* relates to *Sukkot*, for after getting a blessing from *Eisav's* angel and making peace with *Eisav*, the *pasuk* says that *Yaacov* made "sukkot" for his cattle and called the place "Sukkot." (Bereshit 33:17) In the preceding story, at the time he met the angel, we are told that *Yaacov* was alone because he returned to retrieve some small jars he had left behind. The *Talmud* (Chullin 91a) states that possessions, even minor ones, are seen by the righteous as gifts from *Hashem*, and are treasured as such. The time we spend in the *sukkah*, outside of our homes and detached from our everyday luxuries that we take for granted, helps us to learn this lesson that was emphasized by *Yaacov Avinu*.

Each of the *Arba'ah Minim* represents an essential element of man. The *lulav* represents the spine. A Jew should stand straight and tall, proud of his heritage.

Rabbi Shimson Rafael Hirsch - In the *Haftarah* read on *Sukkot*, *Shabbat Chol HaMoed* (Yechezkel 38:18-39:16) describes "Gog" (a nation from "Magog") attacking Israel with the Jews securing victory during the Holiday of *Sukkot*. "Gog" is the Hebrew word for roof, which is a division between man and G-d. The battle between Gog and Israel is really a battle between a roof, which is a rejection of *Hashem* and a *sukkah* which requires the ability to see the stars and, accordingly, recognize *Hashem*. The Nation of Israel is unique in its recognition and connection to *Hashem*. This is demonstrated by the fact that the *gematria* of "גוג ומגוג," "Gog and Magog" is seventy, representing the seventy non-Jewish nations of the world.

5761

Rabbi Yossi Jankovits – The *Gemara* (Sukkah 11b) discusses the dispute between *Rabbi Akiva* and *Rabbi Eliezer* concerning the nature of the *sukkah*. *Rabbi Akiva* states that the *sukkah* represents the actual booths that *Bnei Yisrael* made in the *midbar*, while *Rabbi Eliezer* holds that the *sukkah* commemorates the *Anaini HaKavod* which protected them in the *midbar*. The two options can be reconciled based on the fact that, according to Targum Yonatan (Devarim 25:18), both *Shevat Dan* and the *Erev Rav* were outside of the *Anaini HaKavod* during the desert travels, and presumably survived in *sukkot* while the rest of *Bnei Yisrael* was within the Clouds. The fact that one could survive outside the Clouds also demonstrates that, unlike the *Mon* and the water of *Be'er Miriam*, the *Anaini HaKavod* were not a survival requirement but rather were a *chesed* from *Hashem*. As such, unlike the *Mon* and the *mayim*, the *Anaini HaKavod* were worthy of their own Holiday of *Sukkot*.

The *halachah* of building a *sukkah* is contained in the word itself, סכה. A kosher *sukkah* may have four walls, like a "sameach," ס; three walls, like a "chaf," כ; or two walls and a part of a third, like a "hey," ה.

Rabbi Yossi Jankovits - The *Gemara* (Avodah Zareh 3a) states that in the days of *Moshiach* the nations of the world will petition *Hashem* to allow them to keep the *Torah*, and in response *Hashem* will command them in the *mitzvah* of sukkah. The *goyim* will fail in keeping even this single *mitzvah*, as it will be too hot for them to remain in the *sukkah* and they will trample it in frustration as they leave it. There are many questions one can ask on this enigmatic story. First, there is apparent irrationality in commanding them to sit in a *sukkah* on a hot day. Moreover, why would *Hashem* specifically command the *goyim* in the *mitzvah* of *sukkah*, which *Chazal* (Sukkah 11b) tell us is meant to commemorate the *Anaini Hakavod* in the *midbar*, which benefited only the Jews but not the *Erev Rav*? Does it make sense to command the *goyim* in a *mitzvah* that has no relation to their historical experience? The Satmar Rav answers that a sincere desire to serve *Hashem* should be independent of rational understanding. The *goyim* say "Please command us so that we can serve," yet when commanded they reject the *mitzvah* as irrational and their insincerity is unmasked by their actions. True *Avodat Hashem* treats the *mitzvot* as *chukim*.

5762

Rabbi Yisroel Ciner – *Rabbi Eliezer's* opinion, recorded in the *Gemara* (Sukkah 11b), is that the *sukkot* we build on the Holiday commemorate the *Anaini HaKavod* that protected the Jews in the *midbar*. Yet we know that *Bnei Yisrael* left *Mitzrayim* on 15 *Nissan*, so why do we celebrate *Sukkot* in *Tishrei*? The Jews received the first two *mitzvot* of the *Torah* forty-nine days after the Exodus, on the 6 *Sivan*. *Moshe* then spent forty days on *Har Sinai*, after which the Jews committed the *cheit haeigel* on 17 *Tammuz* and the *Anaini HaKavod* departed. *Moshe* returned to speak with *Hashem* for an additional forty days, and he returned to *Bnei Yisrael* on *Rosh Chodesh Elul*. He ascended for a final forty-day period that culminated in his return on *Yom Kippur*, with his face aglow and full forgiveness for the Jews. It is at that moment that the *Anaini HaKavod* returned, and it is this second version of the Clouds of Glory that we celebrate. The theme of *Sukkot* is reconnection to *Hashem* after error and forgiveness.

Rabbi Yissocher Frand – The Tur (Orach Chayim 417) tells us that the three pilgrimage holidays mandated by the *Torah* correspond to the three *Avot*. *Avraham* represents *Pesach*, as that is the time in which he welcomed the three angels (Rashi on Bereshit 18:10); *Yitzchak* represents *Shavuot*, as the ram's horn from the *Akeidah* was blown at *Matan Torah* (Rashi on Shemot 19:13), which *Shavuot* commemorates; and *Yaacov* represents *Sukkot*, for he made "sukkot" for his livestock. (Bereshit 33:17) The Ohr HaChaim says that *Yaacov* was the first person ever to make shelter for animals, by which he was demonstrating *hakarat hatov*, a *middah* that he passed on to his son *Yosef*. It was this trait, rather than fear of punishment, that ultimately stopped *Yosef* from sinning with *Potiphar's* wife. And this *middah* is strongly connected to the holiday of *Sukkot* when we thank *Hashem* for sustaining us in the *midbar*.

5763

Rabbi Yochanan Zweig –The *Gemara* (Avodah Zareh 3a) tells us that the *goyim* complained to *Hashem* that He did not give them the merit of any *mitzvot*. In response, *Hashem* instructs the *goy* to build a *sukkah* and then He makes the day unbearably hot. The *goy* departs from the *sukkah*, kicking it on the way out. The question arises, what did the *goy* do wrong? Even a Jew would be justified in leaving the *sukkah* under such conditions. The difference is that the Jew would not have kicked the *sukkah*. The *goy* is interested only in the result, and when his objective is not obtained (i.e., he is not able to sit in the *sukkah*), he expresses frustration at the total failure. The Jew appreciates the process, when he knows that building the *sukkah* was an expression of love for *Hashem*, despite the fact that he is unable to sit in it thereafter. Rabbi Zweig uses the example of his wife's cooking for three full days in anticipation of a visit from their married daughter and her family. When the daughter was "snowed-in" and had to cancel her trip, the *Rebbetzi*n didn't kick the refrigerator that held all the prepared food. Both she and her daughter knew all the work was worth it, and worth talking about, as an expression of love.

Rabbi Keith Wasserstrom – The most prevalent custom for waving the *Arba'ah Minim* during *Hallel* on *Sukkot* dictates that for the *pasuk* "הוֹדוּ לַי-י כִּי טוֹב כִּי לְעוֹלָם חַסְדּוֹ," "Give thanks to Hashem for He is Good, His Kindness is Eternal" (Tehillim 136:1), on the word "tov," "good," one points the *lulav* in a backwards direction. This symbolizes that what seems bitter and distressful when it is occurring often is "good" and beneficial in hindsight, when looking in a "backwards" direction.

5764

Rabbi Yoel Caroline – The well-known *Midrash* (Vayikra Rabbah 30:12) characterizes the *aravot* of the *Arba'ah Minim* as having no taste and no smell, which is equated to the service of the simple Jew towards *Hashem*. The Lubavitcher Rebbe indicated that this does not mean such a Jew is devoid of *mitzvot* and *Torah* learning, but rather that he is motivated not by his internal love for *mitzvot* or *Torah* but rather by a pure and simple desire to serve *Hashem*. In actuality, the purest of the *Arba'ah Minim* are the *aravot* and the purest of the Jews are those to whom *aravot* are compared. The idea is not that such Jews are not involved at all in *Avodat Hashem*, but rather they are not compromised by personal pleasure or benefit in the process, receiving no "taste" or "smell" from their efforts.

5765

Rabbi Yossi Jankovits – While the *Gemara* (Sukkah 11) describes the *machloket* between *Rabbi Akiva* and *Rabbi Eliezer* regarding the meaning of *Sukkot*, it seems clear, based on *halachah*, that we follow the opinion of *Rabbi Eliezer*, who holds that the *sukkah* commemorates the *Anaini HaKavod*. For the *halachah* (Orach Chayim 630:2) makes clear that two walls and a portion of a third is adequate for a *sukkah*, which could not be the case if we followed the opinion of *Rabbi Akiva* who holds the *sukkah* commemorates the actual *sukkot* in which the Jews dwelled in the *midbar*. Clearly two and a half walls would be inadequate to maintain modest family living arrangements in the desert.

5766

Rabbi Avraham Twerski – The *sukkah* is representative of our time in this world, which is temporary and fleeting. We must always be mindful that this world is merely an anteroom for the World to Come, *Olam HaEmet*. This is why the *sukkah* may not have any permanence. Nevertheless, we take great pains to adorn the *sukkah* with decorations and we are not permitted to be uncomfortable while living in the *sukkah*. This approach applies in our approach to *Olam HaZeh*. We are not merely permitted but encouraged to enjoy our time in this world and to be as comfortable as possible within the *Torah* and *mitzvot* system that *Hashem* provided us.

5769

Rabbi Joseph B. Soloveitchik – With respect to the *Arba'ah Minim*, we make a *berachah* only on the *lulav*. The *Gemara* (Sukkah 37b) states that as the *lulav* is the tallest of the *Arba'ah Minim*, we learn that receiving *Hashem's* gifts is dependent on "standing tall," apart from the other nations, and cognizant of our worth as the Chosen People. The Rav explains (Yemei Zikaron, pp. 134-35) that this message of Jewish identity and pride is applicable to the Jews in Israel (in how they interact with and try to appease their neighbors), as well as the Jews in the Diaspora, especially America, who all too often sacrifice their children's connection to Jewish identity and pride in the name of conforming to the ways of the *goyim*.

5770

Rabbi Yehudah Prero – The Tur (Orach Chayim 417) writes that each of the *Shalosh Regalim* corresponds to one of the *Avot*: *Pesach* to *Avraham*, *Yitzchak* to *Shavuot* and *Yaacov* to *Sukkot*. After leaving his evil brother *Eisav*, the *Torah* tells us "וַיִּסַּע יַעֲקֹב סֻכֹּתָה וַיִּבֶן לוֹ בָּיִת וּלְמִקְנֵהוּ עָשָׂה סֻכֹּת עַל כֵּן קָרָא שֵׁם הַמָּקוֹם סֻכּוֹת," "And Yaacov traveled to Sukkot and built himself a house, and for his cattle he made sukkot; therefore he named the place Sukkot." (Bereshit 33:17) *Targum Yonatan* (Bereshit 33:17) states that *Yaacov* built a *beit midrash* for himself, and because the *Torah* he would learn there would be to the everlasting merit of *Bnei Yisrael*, that structure had to be permanent. Yet he placed his possessions in temporary structures, and in doing so, taught his descendants a valuable lesson about the essential nature of the Holiday, which acknowledges the fleeting nature of our existence in this world.

5772

Rabbi Joseph B. Soloveitchik – One of the central aspects of the celebration of *Sukkot* in the times of the *Beit HaMikdash* was the *Simchat Beit HaShoeivah*, when water was liberally poured on the *Mizbeach*. (Sukkah

51a, 51b) What is the connection between *mayim* and *Sukkot*? The *Gemara* (Tannit 2b) instructs that the *Torah* reading for *Sukkot* is from Parashat Pinchas (Bamidbar 29: 17-35). The referenced *pasukim* include unusual spellings of certain words. There is an extra "mem" in the word "v'neeskaihem" (Bamidbar 29:19); an extra "yud" in the word "unsa'che'ha" (Bamidbar 29:31); and another extra "mem" in the word "k'mishpatam" (Bamidbar 29:33). Together these letters spell "מים," "water." On *Sukkot*, when the *Beit HaMikdash* stood, we replaced the daily Wine Libations with the Water Libations on the *Mizbeach*. On *Sukkot*, which the *Torah* refers to as "Chag HaAsif," "The Holiday of the Ingathering" (Shemot 23:16), we experience a feeling of luxury and abundance based on our recent harvest of produce. Such a feeling must be tempered by the introduction of a basic, elemental material of life: water.

Rabbi Josef B. Soloveitchik - *Halachah* makes accommodations for the "istanis," a sensitive person. For example, as stated in the *Gemara* (Berachot 16b), during the *Nine Days*, bathing in warm water for pleasure is prohibited, yet bathing in warm water due to personal pain and discomfort is allowed. So too in the case of eating in the *sukkah*, *halachah* states an individual decides for himself whether or not he is comfortable, and if he is not, then he is *patur*. In order to avail oneself of this regime, he must be willing to apply the same principle to others, meaning we must defer to the sensitivities of others and not offend them, even if by an objective standard what upsets them is not considered upsetting. An individual gets to decide what makes him uncomfortable, whether with relation to *mitzvot* or relations with other people. This goes well beyond *Hillel's* well-known maxim, set forth in the *Talmud* (Shabbat 31a), of "that which is offensive to you do not do to others."

5773

Rabbi Yossi Jankovits – *Sukkot* is unique among the *Shalosh Regalim* in having the *Ushpizin* ceremony. Why not also welcome our Forefathers, for example, on *Pesach*? The Zohar (Pinchas: 219b) states that our *Avot* are present in times of *simchah*, and more than any other time of year, during the *Z'man Simchateinu* of *Sukkot* they are formally with us in the *sukkah*. MRF Note: Perhaps it is also true that there is a unique aspect of *simchah* embodied in each of the *Ushpizin* guests that is ascendant during each night of *Sukkot* and which we should try to understand and absorb on that night.

Rabbi Moshe Meir Weiss – There were three major miracles in the *midbar* (the *Be'er Miriam*, the *Mon*, and the *Anaini HaKavod*), yet we only formally commemorate the Clouds (during *Sukkot*). The Chida indicates that the *Be'er Miriam* and the *Mon* came about through complaining, and therefore were not worthy of commemoration, but not so with the Clouds of Glory, for which the holiday of *Sukkot* was established.

SHEMINI ATZERET

5758

The word "atzeret" comes from the Hebrew root "עצר," meaning "hold back," or "restrain." (Rashi on Vayikra 23:36) The seven day holiday of *Sukkot*, is somewhat international in nature, for the *Talmud* (Sukkah 55b) informs us that seventy bulls were offered in the *Beit HaMikdash* for the seventy nations of the world, and even today, many non-Jews come to *Yerushalayim* during *Sukkot*. Following the festivities of *Sukkot*, however, we celebrate *Shemini Atzeret*, a separate holiday whereby *Hashem* tells his Children to "restrain" themselves and tarry in *Yerushalayim* for a private, more intimate encounter with Him. (Rashi on Vayikra 23:36)

5759

The number seven in Judaism denotes both Holiness and completeness as evidenced by the Holy Seventh Day (i.e. *Shabbat*) which completes the seven day week. Yet the number eight represents something more: transcendence (for example, the *brit milah*, which takes place on the eighth day after birth, is a supernatural action in service to *Hashem*). There are seven days of *Pesach* during which we engage in the seven *mitzvot* of the *Seder* (two from the *Torah*: telling the story of the Exodus and eating *matzah*, and five from the Rabbis: eating *maror*, eating *Afikomen*, reciting *Hallel*, drinking four cups of wine and acting as a free man). This is followed by seven weeks of *Sefirat HaOmer*. There are seven days connecting *Rosh Hashanah* to *Yom Kippur*, followed by seven days of *Sukkot*, during which we take *Arba'ah Minim* composed of seven items (one *etrog*, one *lulav*, three *hadassim* and two *aravot*). Shemini Atzeret literally means the "Convocation of the Eighth," and in contrast to other *Yom Tovim* that require performance of physical *mitzvot* (e.g. *Pesach* and *Sukkot*), it is the metaphysical holiday of *Shemini Atzeret* that elevates and completes all the *Yom Tovim* that precede it. In fact, *Shemini Atzeret* is observed as the eighth day of *Yom Tov* counting from *Pesach* (first day of *Pesach* - 1, last day of *Pesach* - 2, *Shavuot* - 3, two days of *Rosh Hashanah* -4, 5, *Yom Kippur* -6 and first day of *Sukkot* - 7).

5760

The *Gemara* (Sukkah 47a) is clear that outside *Eretz Yisrael* one sits in the *sukkah* on *Shemini Atzeret* without making a *berachah*, since there is a *safek* as to whether the day is actually the *Chol HaMoed*, the seventh day of *Sukkot* (requiring dwelling in the *sukkah*) or the *Yom Tov* of *Shemini Atzeret* (when one is prohibited from dwelling in the *sukkah*). Tosafot says saying the *berachah* of Sukkah, which we recite on *Chol HaMoed Sukkot*, would cheapen *Shemini Atzeret*, and we therefore refrain.

5762

In years where there is no *Shabbat Chol HaMoed* for *Sukkot*, we read *Kohelet* on *Shemini Atzeret*. (Orach Chaim 663:2) In the wake of the recent horrific terror attacks on September 11, one passage stands out as particularly apropos. "וְרָאִיתִי אֶת כָּל מַעֲשֵׂה הָאלקים כִּי לֹא יוּכַל הָאָדָם לִמְצוֹא אֶת הַמַּעֲשֶׂה אֲשֶׁר נַעֲשָׂה תַחַת הַשֶּׁמֶשׁ בְּשֶׁל אֲשֶׁר יַעֲמֹל הָאָדָם לְבַקֵּשׁ וְלֹא יִמְצָא וְגַם אִם יֹאמַר הֶחָכָם לָדַעַת לֹא יוּכַל לִמְצֹא," "And I saw all the Deed of G-d, for a person will not be able to understand the Deed that is done under the sun, because though a man toils to seek, he will not understand, and even if the wise man claims to know, he will be unable to understand." (Kohelet 8:17)

5763

Kohelet is read on *Shemini Atzeret* in years where there is no *Shabbat Chol HaMoed*. The *pasuk* states "וְהַחוּט הַמְשֻׁלָּשׁ לֹא בִמְהֵרָה יִנָּתֵק," "and a three-ply rope will not be severed." (Kohelet 4:12) This can mean that when a man, a woman and *Hashem* are found together in a home, the marriage will endure.

5764

Rabbi Yossi Jankovits – The *pasuk* in Parashat Pinchas states "בַּיּוֹם הַשְּׁמִינִי עֲצֶרֶת תִּהְיֶה לָכֶם כָּל מְלֶאכֶת עֲבֹדָה לֹא תַעֲשׂוּ," "On the eighth day <u>will be</u> a time of restriction for you; you shall not perform any mundane work," (Bamidbar 29:35) using the future tense to describe the holiday. There is a *Midrash* (Mishlei: perek 9) that says that in the days of *Mashiach* the only *Yom Tov* that will remain will be *Purim*. There is another *Midrash Rabbah* (Bamidbar 21:23) that states that the future tense used to describe *Shemini Atzeret* indicates that *Hashem* added this holiday purely as a reward for the Jews. The Divrei Yoel explains that currently all *Yom Tovim* are a "zechair l'yitziat Mitzrayim," "a remembrance of the Exodus from Egypt." Yet the *Gemara* (Berachot 12b) relates that in the times of *Mashiach* the second *geulah* will overshadow the first, and therefore the holidays will be kept not to remember the first *geulah* but simply because they are gifts commanded by *Hashem*. This is actually a return to the original way in which the *Talmud* (Yoma 28b) informs us that *Avraham Avinu* observed all the *Yom Tovim* prior to *Matan Torah* and the Exodus, which was keeping *Yom Tov* only for the *Yom Tov's* sake. Of all the *Yom Tovim*, *Shemini Atzeret* is most focused upon simple observance unconnected to any historical event, and, as such, it is well-suited for the days of *Mashiach*. Incidentally, Shem MiShmuel (Purim 5677) indicates that *Purim*, which commemorates the Jews' victory over *Amalek*, will be sustained as a *Yom Tov* because the celebration of the victory over *Amalek* will continue even after *Mashiach's* arrival.

5765

Rabbi Edward Davis – There is a *mashal* that describes the transition we make from *Elul*, through the *Yom Tov* season to *Shemini Atzeret* and beyond. There was once a king who sent his daughter to a far away country to marry its prince. The prince was abusive and the princess longed to again be near her father. One day the king announced he intended to visit the couple. Immediately the prince began treating the princess better. By the time the king arrived the princess was again healthy and happy. When the time came for the king to leave, the princess begged him to remain, so that she should not again be subject to abuse. The king decreed that the couple should move and live closer to the king to allow for more frequent visits, and in this way, the princess would always be well-cared for. The princess in the story is our *neshamah*, and the prince is our *guf*, which regularly "abuses" our soul pursuing the physical and material things of this world. Beginning in *Elul*, the "King," *Hashem*, draws closer, and throughout the *Yom Tovim*, the "princess" delights in the presence of the "King." The "visit" culminates on *Sukkot*, when we move to the *Sukkah* and our *neshamah* rejoices in the spirituality that replaces the physicality and allows for an even greater connection to the King. As the King's visit is coming to an end, we seek a lingering, continuing closeness to the King on *Shemini Atzeret*, and we resolve, through *Torah* study and *maasim tovim*, to "move closer" to Him throughout the new year.

5770

Rabbi Yisroel Ciner - The Tur (Orach Chayim 417) tells us that the *Shalosh Regalim* correspond to the three *Avot*. *Avraham* represents *Pesach*, as that is the time in which he welcomed the three angels (Rashi on Bereshit 18:10); *Yitzchak* represents *Shavuot*, as the ram's horn from the *Akeidah* was blown at *Matan Torah* (Rashi on Shemot 19:13), which *Shavuot* commemorates; and *Yaacov* represents *Sukkot*, for he made "sukkot" for his livestock. (Bereshit 33:17) The holiday of *Sukkot* involved the offering of seventy bulls, which the *Gemara* (Sukkah 55b) tells us are brought on behalf of the seventy nations of the world. *Shemini Atzeret* is also a *Chag*, a *Yom Tov*, separate and distinct from *Sukkot*, which precedes it. Unlike *Sukkot*, *Shemini Atzeret* is a much more intimate assembly, meant to be shared only between *Hashem* and His Chosen People. (Rashi on Vayikra 23:36) The Lubavitcher Rebbe (Likutei Sichot 3:832), quoting the Zohar, states that, based on the same theme, *Shemini Atzeret* corresponds to *Yosef HaTzaddik*, who is often regarded as having been elevated by his father *Yaacov* to the level of "Fourth" of the *Avot*. (see Bereshit 48:5) The *Torah* tells us "וְלֹא יָכֹל יוֹסֵף לְהִתְאַפֵּק לְכֹל הַנִּצָּבִים עָלָיו וַיִּקְרָא הוֹצִיאוּ כָל אִישׁ מֵעָלָי וְלֹא עָמַד אִישׁ אִתּוֹ בְּהִתְוַדַּע יוֹסֵף אֶל אֶחָיו," "Now Yosef could not restrain himself in the presence of all those standing before him, and he called out, 'Take out everyone away from me!' And no [outsider] stood with him when Yosef made himself known to his Brothers," (Bereshit 45:1) which is thematically linked to removing the seventy nations to allow "family time" only with *Hashem*. *Shemini Atzeret* also corresponds to the World to Come, as the number seven (i.e. the days of Sukkot) represents nature and the apparent world, and the eighth day signifies the supernatural and the revelation of what is hidden. Similarly, it was *Yosef* that revealed himself to his Brothers and provided immediate clarity and understanding of a previously confused reality. (Bereshit 45:3)

5771

Dubner Maggid – Once a wealthy merchant returned from a long business trip with many presents for his stepchildren and none for his kids. He explained to his birth children that he wanted to endear the stepchildren to him by giving them gifts, but that the mere fact of his return after an extended absence should be enough for his own children. The *Talmud* (Sukkah 55b) tells us that on *Sukkot Bnei Yisrael* offered seventy bulls corresponding to the seventy nations of the world, but on *Shemini Atzeret* only one bull was brought. The close relationship shared between the Jews and *Hashem* is our lasting gift, more precious than any sacrifices could be.

5772

Reb Aaron Moses – Rabbi David Sutton, in the name of Rabbi Shimon Schwab, tells us that we are given a formula in our *davening* for how to retain our closeness to *Hashem* and achieve greater spirituality following *Shemini Atzeret* and the conclusion of the *Yom Tovim*. Beginning *Mussaf* on *Shemini Atzeret* we add "משיב הרוח ומוריד הגשם," "[Hashem] makes the wind blow and makes the rain fall." "Mashiv" is from the *shoresh* "תשוב," meaning "to return or repeat," and "ruach" means "spirituality." "Morid" means "to reduce" and "geshem" is related to the word "גַשְׁמִי," "physicality."

The *pasuk* can therefore be translated to reveal the secret to maintaining the elevated feeling of closeness to *Hashem* that prevails during the *Yom Tovim* of *Tishrei*: "Return to the spiritual and reduce the physical," a simple yet powerful prescription.

5773

Rabbi Herschel Schachter – The prohibition of getting married on *Yom Tov* is based on the principle set forth in the *Talmud Yerushalmi* (Moed Katan 1:7) of "אין מערבין שמחה בשמחה," "we do not mix one happiness with another happiness," which itself is derived from the *Torah* narrative when *Lavan* told *Yaacov* to wait a week following his marriage to *Leah* before marrying *Rachel*. (Bereshit 29:27) On *Yom Tov* we are therefore prohibited from adding the *simchah* connected to a wedding to the *simchah* of the holiday. Incidentally, the prohibition of getting married on *Shabbat* has a different source, for unlike *Yom Tov*, *Shabbat* does not contain *simchah* but rather *oneg*, which is "joy." The Sages prohibited weddings on *Shabbat* based on the Rambam (Hilchot Ishut 10:14) citing the *issur* of "mekach u'memkar," "buying and selling," since a marriage ceremony is akin to a business transaction and the Sages were concerned one would come to write a document. Based on the *inyan* of אין מערבין שמחה בשמחה we might have been concerned that a *siyum* of the *Torah* would be prohibited on *Yom Tov*, yet we know that this is the custom on *Shemini Atzeret* in *Eretz Yisrael* (and on *Simchat Torah* in *chutz l'Aretz*). *Shemini Atzeret* is a *Yom Tov* that is distinct from *Sukkot* which precedes it (hence the recitation of *Shehecheyanu*, which is not the case on the final day(s) of *Pesach*), and therefore the *simchah* of *Shemini Atzeret* must be distinct in some way from the *simchah* of *Sukkot*. Rashi tells us that after all the activity of *Sukkot* *Hashem* asks His Children to tarry for one more day based on the fact that we are beloved and special to Him. (Rashi on Vayikra 23:36) The *simchah* of *Shemini Atzeret*, therefore, is the happiness in being the *Am HaNivchar*," the "Chosen Nation" of *Hashem*. Yet what is it that makes *Am Yisrael* the *Am HaNivchar*? Of course it is our acceptance of His Holy

Torah. Therefore, the *simchah* contained in the *Torah's* completion does not compete with the *simchah* of celebrating Our unique status, but rather it aligns with and enhances it.

SIMCHAT TORAH

5760

Dubner Maggid - The interplay between *Shavuot*, the Time of Giving of the *Torah*, and *Simchat Torah*, a part of the Time of Our Happiness, is demonstrated through a *mashal* of a king who wanted to marry off his daughter "sight unseen." No one would assume the risk of taking the girl except for one man who loved the king very much and reasoned that anyone coming from him would be just as lovable. The groom celebrated well on the day of his engagement but danced deliriously months later at his wedding, when he saw the immeasurable beauty of his new bride. *Bnei Yisrael* is the groom in the story. On *Shavuot* we said "naaseh v'nishmah," "we will do it and then learn it." We accepted the *Torah*, our bride, without condition, because we know our Father, the King, *Hashem*, loves us and only wants good for us. Months later, when *Simchat Torah* arrives, we are able to rejoice at an even higher level, having spent many months living with our precious Bride.

The Vilna Gaon – There is irony in the fact that we read from Parashat VeZot HaBerachah about the death of *Moshe Rabbeinu* on *Simchat Torah*, the very day we rejoice in the *Torah* that he gave us. Similarly, of all the *parshiot* from Moshe's birth at the beginning of *Sefer Shemot* to his death at the end of *Sefer Devarim*, Parashat Tetzaveh is the only one where *Moshe's* name does not appear. The *Gemara* (Kiddushin 38a) states that *Moshe* died on 7 *Adar*, which usually falls out during the week Parashat Tetzaveh is read. Rather than viewing the omission in a negative light, in removing his name, *Hashem* was, in fact, paying *Moshe*, the teacher <u>par excellence</u> of *Bnei Yisrael*, the highest compliment. A teacher is regarded as most effective when his pupils perform on their own, absent the teacher's involvement. *Bnei Yisrael* had become attached to *Hashem's Torah*, rather than *Moshe's* cult of personality. This had come about, in part, due to *Moshe's* speech impediment (Shemot 4:10, 6:12 and 6:30), which ensured that the content of his words, not their delivery, would matter most. So both the omission of *Moshe's* name in the week of his *yahrzeit* and the mention of his death at the time we celebrate his *Torah* are each a tribute to *Moshe*, and a part of his unparalleled legacy as the greatest leader of *Am Yisrael*.

5761

Rabbi Yechezkel Abramsky - On *Simchat Torah* (or on *Shemini Atzeret* in *Eretz Yisrael*) we read the *Haftarah* from *Sefer Yehoshua* that three times uses the expression "חֲזַק וֶאֱמָץ," "be strong and have courage." (Yehoshua 1: 1-18) *Hashem* adjures *Yehoshua* once with regard to waging war against the thirty-one kings of *Eretz Yisrael*, and twice in encouraging *Yehoshua* to stay true to the *Torah* and *mitzvot* his *Rebbe*, *Moshe Rabbeinu*, had taught him. From here we see that greater strength and courage is needed to maintain the spiritual goals of Judaism than is required to physically conquer a country.

5763

Rabbi Eliyahu KiTov – The relationship of *Sukkot* to *Shemini Atzeret/ Simchat Torah* is similar to the relationship between *Pesach* to *Shavuot*. On *Pesach Bnei Yisrael* emerged free of *Paroh* and slavery, and thereafter prepared forty-nine days to receive the *Torah* through an "atzeret," or "assembly" on *Shavuot*. On *Yom Kippur* we emerge free of sin and prepare seven days over *Sukkot* to properly rejoice with the *Torah* through the *atzeret* of *Simchat Torah*. The first assembly of *Shavuot*, which incidentally, the *Gemara* calls "Atzeret," celebrates the initial freedom of the body (on *Pesach*) transforming into fear and awe of *Hashem* as manifested on *Shavuot*. The second assembly of *Simchat Torah* celebrates the initial freedom of the soul on *Yom Kippur*, transforming into joy and love for *Hashem* as manifested on *Simchat Torah*. In both cases, with the passage of time, the *atzeret*, in combination with the *Torah*, seals the covenant made between *Bnei Yisrael* and *Hashem*. In fact, for perfect symmetry, it would have made sense to wait fifty days from *Yom Kippur* to *Simchat Torah*, but that would have pushed *Shemini Atzeret* to the dead of winter.

5764

Rabbi Shmuel Butman – The month of *Tishrei* has been compared to an annual trade fair at which a merchant purchases merchandise with which to conduct his business the entire year. Upon returning home, he unpacks his wares to take stock of what he has obtained to sustain himself for the upcoming year. *Simchat Torah* is our final opportunity to "grab" the Holiness and power of the *Yom Tov* season with which to spiritually sustain ourselves for the ensuing long, cold winter and beyond.

5765

Rabbi Yoel Pomerantz - The *simchah* one attains as a result of learning *Torah* is an unadulterated, pure form of joy. The *Gemara* (Berachot 8a) states והיינו דאמר ר' חייא בר אמי משמיה דעולא מיום שחרב בית המקדש אין לו "להקב"ה בעולמו אלא ארבע אמות של הלכה בלבד," "And this is what Rabbi Chiyya bar Ami said in the name of Ulla: 'Since the day the Beit Mikdash was destroyed, the only Place for [Hashem's Presence] to reside is the four cubits of Torah law.'" The *Talmud* (Shabbat 30b) states that the *Shechinah* can only manifest Itself where there is joy, and that the only environment that fits this description in *Olam HaZeh* is a place where *Torah* is studied.

Rabbi Yossi Jankovits – On Simchat Torah we conclude the reading of the *Torah* with the final *pasuk* which mentions "וּלְכֹל הַיָּד הַחֲזָקָה וּלְכֹל הַמּוֹרָא הַגָּדוֹל אֲשֶׁר עָשָׂה מֹשֶׁה לְעֵינֵי כָּל יִשְׂרָאֵל," "and all the strong hand, and all the great awe, which Moshe performed before the eyes of all Israel." (Devarim 34:12) Rashi on this *pasuk* says the *Torah* is referring to the smashing of the original *Luchot*, which the *Gemara* (Shabbat 87a) states *Hashem* considered *Moshe's* greatest achievement. Yet the *Gemara* (Eruvin 54a) also tells us that *Moshe's* act of smashing these *Luchot* brought forgetfulness to the world, which could suggest a negative result. In truth, because of the fact that *Torah* learning is soon forgotten, *Bnei Yisrael* is required on *Simchat Torah* to begin again and learn the *Torah* anew from its beginning, immediately after we conclude reading it.

5770

Rabbi Yehudah Prero – With regard to the primary *kaylim* of the *Mishkan*, *Hashem* commanded *Moshe* individually to create both the *Shulchan* (Shemot 25:23) and the *Menorah* (Shemot 25:31), but for the *Aron*, which housed the *Luchot* which represent the Holy *Torah*, *Hashem* commanded that "they," (i.e. all of *Bnei Yisrael*) should make it. (Shemot 25:10) This demonstrates that every Jew has a portion in the *Torah*, an idea that is manifested in the *minhag* that everyone in *shul* on *Simchat Torah* receives an *aliyah*.

Vilna Gaon – There is a debate in the *Gemara* (Gittin 60a) as to whether, if *Hashem* revealed the entire *Torah* to *Moshe* at *Har Sinai*, *Moshe* himself wrote the narrative of his own death, as recorded at the end of Parashat VeZot HaBerachah. (Devarim 34:5-12) The Vilna Gaon indicates that the *Torah* was, indeed, given to *Moshe*, but as one long "run-on sentence" that was "decoded" over time. In this way, *Moshe* would not have known of his death until the end of the forty year period. Read in this manner, the fact that it was, as *Rabbi Shimon* states in the *Gemara* (Bava Batra 15a), written by *Moshe* "בדמע‎," "with tears [of sadness]," could be read not as "with a tear," but rather "mixed-up," meaning unclear, until the very end.

5771

Rabbi Shlomo Riskin – There are three holidays associated with the *Torah*. *Shavuot* celebrates the Giving of the original *Luchot* and the Divine Sinaitic Experience. According to the Beis HaLevi (chelek 2: drosh 18), had *Bnei Yisrael* merited it, the *Torah Shebichtav* would have been the sole *Torah*, because the *Oral Law* would have been included in the *Written Law*. The Talmud (Taanit 30b) tells us that *Yom Kippur* is the day on which the second *Luchot* were received. Unlike the first *Luchot*, which *Hashem* Himself produced, the second *Luchot* were carved by *Moshe*, representing the partnership of G-d and man as manifested in the *Torah Shebaal Peh*. The third holiday is *Simchat Torah*, which represents the broader perfection of all mankind, characterized by our dancing with the *Torah* in public.

The Brisker Rav – On *Simchat Torah* we read the last *parashah* of the *Torah*. The *Gemara* (Menachot 30a) tells us the manner by which *Hashem* conveyed the last eight verses of the *Torah* differed from the way he generally conveyed the text. The normal process was that *Hashem* spoke the words to *Moshe* and he would repeat them, then later write them into a *Torah* scroll. But with the verses about his own death, *Moshe* wordlessly recorded *Hashem's* dictation. This is similar to the distinction between the writing of the *Naviim*, which *Hashem* commanded each respective *navi* to write, and the *Ketuvim*, which Hashem told the *navi* to record so that another could read it at a later date. Here, *Moshe* could record the verses describing his death, although they had not happened, and could then present a complete *sefer* to *Yehoshua*.

5772

Rabbi Shimon Schwab – Upon completing Parashat VeZot HaBerachah, the final *parashah* of the *Torah*, we are happy and immediately begin to learn Parashat Bereshit, the initial *parashah* of the *Torah*. We then enjoy a celebratory feast, typical for a *siyum*. This *minhag* is sourced in the incident of *Shlomo HaMelech* at *Givon* (I Melachim 3:4-15), when *Hashem* directs *Shlomo* to ask for whatever he wishes. Rather than asking for longevity or riches, *Shlomo* responds "וְנָתַתָּ לְעַבְדְּךָ לֵב שֹׁמֵעַ לִשְׁפֹּט אֶת עַמְּךָ לְהָבִין בֵּין טוֹב לְרָע כִּי מִי יוּכַל לִשְׁפֹּט אֶת עַמְּךָ הַכָּבֵד הַזֶּה," "Give Your servant an understanding heart to judge Your Nation, that I may discern between good and bad; for who is able to judge this Your great Nation?" (I Melachim 3:9) *Hashem* was pleased with *Shlomo's* request and granted him his wish, after which *Shlomo* made a great feast. (I Melachim 3:15) This seems contrary to the concept of a *siyum*, which ostensibly is a celebration of having completed a segment of *Torah* learning. In this case, *Shlomo* had not completed any *Torah* learning, but rather had committed himself to return to his learning armed with the greater expertise and clearer vision that *Hashem* had just recently granted him. This is precisely what is described in the *Hadran Alach* of a *siyum* that immediately precedes a *seudat mitzvah*, which includes language focused on applying the newly acquired *Torah* knowledge to continuing to learn. This never-ending commitment to *Torah* learning is what *Shlomo* was celebrating and what we celebrate as a Nation on *Simchat Torah*.

CHANUKAH

5758

It is well known that following their dramatic victory over the Greeks, the Jews found a cruse of oil in the *Beit HaMikdash* sufficient to burn for one day but which miraculously burned for eight. A classic question of the Beit Yosef (Orach Chayim 670) is why, if the flame miraculously burned for seven extra days, do we celebrate eight nights as a holiday? One answer is that finding of the oil in the destroyed Temple was itself an independent miracle that, when combined with the seven additional nights, warrants an eight day celebration. Another answer is that the original cruse was divided into eight equal portions, each of which was lit on a successive night and burned throughout that night.

Tzror Hamor – Why may only "shemen zayit zach, katit lamaor" "pure, crushed olive oil," be used in lighting the Menorah in the *Beit HaMikdash*? (Shemot 27:20) The oil may be compared to *Bnei Yisrael*. Both must be crushed to be at their finest and both separate and inevitably "rise to the top." Even when faced with great difficulties, *Bnei Yisrael* separates out and rises, remaining distinct from the other nations.

5759

Chanukah, the Festival of Lights, is celebrated on the twenty fifth day of *Kislev* and the twenty fifth word of the Torah is "אור," "light." (Bereshit 1:3) Furthermore, we light a total of thirty six candles over the eight nights of *Chanukah* (1+2+3 . . .) and Sefer HaRokeach says that there are thirty six references to light in the *Chumash*.

Iturei Torah – The Torah Temimah points out a connection between *Chanukah* and Parashat Mikeitz, which is almost always read on *Chanukah*. Mikeitz has 2025 words. The *gematria* of the word "ner," "candle," is 250. There are eight days of *Chanukah*, which starts on the twenty-fifth day of the month of *Kislev*. Eight times 250 equals 2000, plus 25 equals 2025!

5760

Vedibarta Bam - We can obtain a deeper understanding of the essence of any Jewish holiday by examining the customs of that day. It is interesting to note the differences in how we celebrate *Purim* and *Chanukah*. On *Purim* we spin the *grogger* from below, which signifies that man, rather than *Hashem*, seems to be directing the story. And indeed, our Rabbis note that *Megillat Esther* appears to document a series of coincidental events and in which *Hashem's* Name does not appear even once. The story of *Purim* involves a National *teshuvah* among *Bnei Yisrael*, something we had to undertake and which *Hashem* could not do for us. Contrast this with the *dreidel* we take on *Chanukah*, which is spun from above. The *dreidel* signifies that *Hashem* is directing the narrative, and the story of *Chanukah* makes clear that when many of *Bnei Yisrael* were assimilating and the Nation was generally undeserving of redemption, *Hashem* nonetheless brought about a great, unnatural miracle for the Jews.

Rabbi Yissocher Frand – The *Midrash* Yalkut Shimoni (Melachim 184) tells us that on the twenty fifth of *Kislev* the preparations for assembly of the *Mishkan* were completed, and that therefore on that day we should celebrate this in addition to *Chanukah*. Yet we could question why we celebrate the Mishkan which was not ultimately erected until the first of *Nissan*, more than three months later. (Shemot 40:1) We learn from this that in Judaism we celebrate our human efforts, not the results, which are ultimately in *Hashem's* Hands.

5761

Rabbi Akiva Tatz – The נר, candle, is central to the celebration of *Chanukah*. The Vilna Gaon quoted the *Kabbalists* who state that נר stands for "nefesh" and "ruach," the lowest and second lowest levels of the human soul. The *nefesh* connects the spiritual self of the soul to the physical self of the body. The *ruach* is the loftier spirit above the *nefesh*. The connection of *nefesh* and *ruach* is unique to humans. The highest level of an animal is *nefesh*, and the lowest level of an angel is *ruach*. On *Chanukah* we celebrate our singular status and ability to merge the spiritual and physical for the betterment of the world.

On *Chanukah* we light olive oil, which the *Navi* (Yirmiyahu 11:16) indicates represents the Jewish People. Like olives, when *Bnei* Yisrael are "crushed" by their oppressors they produce their most beautiful and lasting product. This is alluded to in the *pasuk* which describes what happened when Egypt increased the labor of *Bnei Yisrael*: "וְכַאֲשֶׁר יְעַנּוּ אֹתוֹ כֵּן יִרְבֶּה וְכֵן יִפְרֹץ וַיָּקֻצוּ מִפְּנֵי בְּנֵי יִשְׂרָאֵל," "But as much as [Egypt] would afflict [the Jews], so did they multiply and so did they gain strength, and they were disgusted because of the Children of Israel." (Shemot 1:12) The words "יִרְבֶּה," "increase" and "יִפְרֹץ," "strengthen" are written in the future tense, indicating that it shall be an indelible quality of *Bnei Yisrael* to grow more powerful in time of affliction. Rabbi Meir Shapiro finds this same quality in the roasted egg on the *Seder* plate. Unlike other foods that grow softer with prolonged boiling, the egg hardens. Unlike other nations that grow weak when tested, the Jewish Nation only grows stronger.

5762

Rabbi Tzvi Nightingale – *Chanukah* is a celebration of the triumph of Jewish philosophy over the Greek way of life. Yet the *Gemara* in many ways recognizes the Greek language as an acceptable alternative to Hebrew. For example, one may write a *Sefer Torah* in the Greek language (Megillah 8b) and speak Greek in *Eretz Yisrael*. (Megillah 9b) Furthermore, *Chazal* understood that the Greeks contributed significantly in all areas of secular human civilization. (Bava Kama 82b) If so, what makes Greek philosophy *assur*? For the Greeks, the drive for advancement through competition left no room for righteousness, in stark distinction to *Yiddishkeit*, which has a moral foundation. The distinction is subtle but fundamental. The Hebrew word for Greece is יון, and the spiritual essence of *Bnei Yisrael* is ציון. The minor addition of a "tzadi," representing "צְדִיקוּת," "righteousness," makes a major distinction between the two world views. MRF Note: This *middah* of displaying righteousness rather than competitiveness is exemplified in the humility of *Menashe* despite being passed over by his grandfather *Yaacov* in favor of his younger brother *Ephraim*. (Bereshit 48:13-20)

5763

Sefer Yossifun - The Jews who rebelled against the Syrian-Greeks adopted the moniker "Maccabi," an acronym from the first four words of the *pasuk* in *Torah* "מִי כָמֹכָה בָּאֵלִם ה' מִי כָּמֹכָה נֶאְדָּר בַּקֹּדֶשׁ נוֹרָא תְהִלֹּת עֹשֵׂה פֶלֶא," "Who is like You among the powerful, Hashem? Who is like You, powerful in the Holy place? Too awesome for praises, performing wonders." (Shemot 15:11)

5764

Rabbi Eli Mansour – The Mishnah Berurah (Orach Chayim 677:2) holds that a man who is traveling may fulfill his obligation to light the *Chanukah* lights by having his wife light for him at home. This is because the *mitzvah* of lighting is upon the household and not the individual. One explanation for the uniqueness of the *mitzvah* is that the Greeks ordered the removal of the doors of Jewish homes for the same reason they outlawed *brit milah*. They were attempting to destroy the sanctity and Holiness of the Jewish home, which is the source in the Jewish People. We celebrate our victory over the Greeks and their evil decrees by reasserting the sanctity of the Jewish Home in attaching the *mitzvah* of lighting to the home itself.

Rabbi Eli Mansour – The connection between *Chanukah* and Parashat Mikeitz, which is nearly always read on *Shabbat Chanukah*, is clear. The improbability of the skinny cows swallowing the fat cows without any change in appearance (Bereshit 41:20, 21) is mirrored by the *Chanukah* victory of the *Torah*-true Jews over powerful armies and influences.

5765

Rabbi Edward Davis – *Chanukah* celebrates the discovery of a single cruse of oil that had not been "defiled" by the Greeks. Yet this begs a question: how can oil be ritually defiled? After all, it is not treated like wine, which the Shulchan Aruch (Yoreh Deah 123:1) tells us becomes *halachically* unusable if opened and touched by a *goy*. Homiletically, oil used in the *Menorah* is symbolic of *Torah* wisdom; the proverbial "light of knowledge." The wisdom of the Greeks, although impressive, was inconsistent with the *Torah* based on having been pursued for its own sake and not for the purpose of serving *Hashem*. It was therefore considered "defiled" and unusable by the Jewish People.

5767

Rabbi Yossi Jankovits – Parashat Mikeitz is almost always read on *Shabbat Chanukah*. There is an allusion to the holiday in the *pasuk* describing *Yosef's* delight at seeing his brother *Binyamin* together with his other ten Brothers. "וַיַּרְא יוֹסֵף אִתָּם אֶת בִּנְיָמִין וַיֹּאמֶר לַאֲשֶׁר עַל בֵּיתוֹ הָבֵא אֶת הָאֲנָשִׁים הַבָּיְתָה וּטְבֹחַ טֶבַח וְהָכֵן כִּי אִתִּי יֹאכְלוּ הָאֲנָשִׁים בַּצָּהֳרָיִם," "And Yosef saw Binyamin with them, and he said to the overseer of his house, 'Bring the men into the house and have meat slaughtered and prepare it, for the men will eat with me at noon.'" (Bereshit 43:16) The letter ח, from טבח, combines with the four letters of והכן to form the word חנוכה. Similarly, we know the word "הכן," "prepare," is often used in reference to *Shabbat*. (Shemot 16:5) The lesson is that when all of *Bnei Yisrael* is united there will be a "Chanukah," a "dedication" of the third and final *Beit HaMikdash*, and a *Shabbat* with the coming of the *Mashiach*, may they both happen speedily, and in our day. Amen!

Rabbi Yossi Jankovits – In the traditional *Chanukah* story set forth in Sefer Yossifun, *Matityahu ben Yochanan HaKohein* exclaims the inspirational words "מִי לַיהֹוָה אֵלָי," "Whoever is with Hashem, come to me!," echoing the exact declaration of *Moshe* in Parashat Ki Tisa in connection with the sin of the golden calf. There the text is silent on the question as to whether *Shevet Levy* participated in the *cheit*, or even simply stood by in silence as it took place. And yet, the *pasuk* tells us that after the sin, "וַיַּעֲמֹד מֹשֶׁה בְּשַׁעַר הַמַּחֲנֶה וַיֹּאמֶר מִי לַיהֹוָה אֵלָי וַיֵּאָסְפוּ אֵלָיו כָּל בְּנֵי לֵוִי," "Moshe stood in the gate of the camp and said: 'Whoever is for Hashem, [come] to me!' And all the sons of Levy gathered around him." (Shemot 32:26) More than merely joining *Moshe*, we are told the Tribe of *Levy* took up arms to kill their offending brethren. (Shemot 32:28) Similarly, we are not informed as to the degree to which those Jews who ultimately joined *Matityahu* were earlier complicitous in or apathetic towards the abandonment of *Torah* and the mass assimilation into the Greek-Syrian culture. Regardless, when their *Rebbe* pointed out the seriousness of the situation and demanded immediate *teshuvah*, they responded and made the right choice. The lesson in both cases may be that where the members of *Bnei Yisrael* might have engaged in prohibited acts up to that point, at the moment their *Rebbe* demanded *teshuvah*, some responded and were saved, and many others were slaughtered in a civil war. The message for all of us is clear: when we are made aware of our sinful acts by the wise persons around us, we must take heed and save ourselves from the penalties associated with sinning <u>and</u> failing to listen to the Sages.

5768

Rabbi Berel Wein – During the eight days of *Chanukah* we read from Parashat Nasso which describes the dedication of the *Mishkan* and the gifts brought by the twelve Tribal Leaders, which included *Ephraim* and *Menashe* but excluded *Levy*, the Tribe of *Moshe* and *Aharon*. (Bamidbar 7:1-49) Parashat Behaalotecha, which immediately follows the description of the *Mishkan* dedication, begins with the following pasukim: "'וַיְדַבֵּר ה׳ אֶל מֹשֶׁה לֵּאמֹר דַּבֵּר אֶל אַהֲרֹן וְאָמַרְתָּ אֵלָיו בְּהַעֲלֹתְךָ אֶת הַנֵּרֹת אֶל מוּל פְּנֵי הַמְּנוֹרָה יָאִירוּ שִׁבְעַת הַנֵּרוֹת," "Hashem spoke to Moshe Saying: 'speak to Aharon and say to him: "When you light the lamps, the seven lamps shall cast their light toward the face of the Menorah."'" (Bamidbar 8:1, 2) Rashi notes the proximity in the narrative between the gifts to the *Mishkan* of the Tribal Leaders and *Aharon's mitzvah* of lighting the *Menorah*. "לפי שכשראה אהרן חנוכת הנשיאים חלשה דעתו, שלא היה עמהם בחנוכה, לא הוא ולא שבטו, אמר לו הקב"ה חייך, שלך גדולה משלהם, שאתה מדליק ומטיב את הנרות," "When Aharon saw the dedication [offerings] of the Leaders, he felt distressed over not joining them in this dedication-neither he nor his Tribe. So The Holy One said to him, 'By your life, your [portion] is greater than theirs, for you will light and prepare the lamps.'" (Rashi on Bamidbar 8:2) The Ramban (Bamidbar 8:2) states that references to dedicating the *Mishkan* and lighting of the *Menorah* create strong connections to the holiday of *Chanukah*. Through these *pasukim* Hashem assures *Bnei Yisrael* that our portion is greater than those of the other nations of the world, because every year we will kindle the *Chanukah* lamps and they will not.

5769

Rabbi Edward Davis – On *Chanukah* we recite the poem *Maoz Tzur*, which was authored by "Mordechai" whose name appears as an acrostic. While we usually recite only the first and fifth stanzas, there is significance in all six. Each describes a period of difficulty for the Jewish People, including the travails in *Mitzrayim* (second stanza) and the *Purim* story (fourth stanza) and the mighty deeds and miracles that *Hashem* performed on our behalf. A question naturally arises as to why we only recite *Maoz Tzur* on *Chanukah* and not also *Pesach* and *Purim*? If the intent is to recall the Power and *Chesed* of *Hashem*, it would also seem appropriate for those other holidays. Perhaps the answer is that there is an express mention in both the *Haggadah* and the *Megillah* of the obligation of future generations to recount the Great Deeds that *Hashem* performed on our behalf. The *Al HaNisim* prayer recited on *Chanukah* does not contain any such mention, and so it is therefore fitting on *Chanukah* alone to supplement our prayers with the recitation of *Maoz Tzur*.

5770

Reb Yossi Hahn – The essence of *Chanukah* is thanksgiving, not necessarily lighting a *chanukiah* or publicizing the miracles that occurred, which are really tools towards prompting *Bnei Yisrael* to give thanks to *Hashem*. The *Al HaNisim* prayer appears in the "Modim," or "Thanksgiving" section of the *Shemoneh Esrei* and contains the language "וְקָבְעוּ שְׁמוֹנַת יְמֵי חֲנֻכָּה אֵלּוּ לְהוֹדוֹת וּלְהַלֵּל לְשִׁמְךָ הַגָּדוֹל," "and [the Rabbis] established eight days of dedication for great thanksgiving and praise." While the great military victory and the kindling of the lights are mentioned, the resulting primary obligation is clearly gratitude.

5771

Rabbi Yaakov Klass – The Ta'amei HaMinhagim, in the name of the Chasam Sofer, states that there is not a full discussion of *Chanukah* found in the *Mishnah* because *Rabbi Yehudah HaNasi*, that redactor of the *Mishnah* and a descendant of *David HaMelech*, became angry when the *Maccabim*, who were from the Tribe of *Levy*, took control of Kingship of *Am Yisrael*. This violated *Hashem's* express Edict that the kingship would forever remain in the line of *Yehudah* and King David. (Bereshit 49:10)

5772

Rabbi Yosef Weinstock – There is a common link between the story of *Yosef* and the story of *Chanukah*. Both represent incomplete victory. *Yosef* overcame the challenge of *Potiphar's* wife, and ultimately saved *Yaacov* and his Sons. Yet *Yosef* also ushered in the enslavement of *Mitzrayim*. The *Talmud* (Sukkah 32a) tells us that in the future *Mashiach ben Yosef* will initiate the Final Redemption, but will die and make way for *Mashiach ben David*, who will bring about the final victory. So too, *Chanukah* was a victory that ultimately gave way to the *Chashmonaim*, who were *Kohanim*, unjustly retaining the power of the Jewish kingship which rightfully rested in the Tribe of *Yehudah*. Ramban (Bereshit 49:10) states that this resulted in the destruction of the Second Temple, which awaits rebuilding by *Mashiach ben David*. While both stories provide a sobering understanding that victory is fleeting and that ultimate goodness remains elusive until the *Geulah*, each story also teaches us that it is appropriate to celebrate the seemingly good that comes our way, even if it doesn't ultimately endure.

Rabbi Akiva Tatz – The philosophy of the Greeks contrasts starkly from that of the Jews. While *Yiddishkeit* focuses on elevating man from the mundane to the Heavenly, the Greek approach is the triumph of the physical, nature-based over the spiritual, as represented by the Hebrew word for Greece: יון. Reading right to left, the letters, "yud," "vav," "nun," show a physical progression from high to low. The *yud* (י) is above the line, closer to Heaven. The *vav* (ו) represents a *yud* pulled downwards towards earth, and the *nun sofit* (ן) goes even lower still, representing the decline of society from the lofty to the base. MRF Note: This recalls Winston Churchill's famous speech, given immediately after World War II in 1946, in which he lamented that "an Iron Curtain has descended across the continent," in the form of Soviet influence. Indeed, the word יון depicts a curtain of physicality descending in stages.

5773

Rabbi Moshe Parnes – There is a well-known question of why we celebrate eight days of *Chanukah*. Clearly if the single cruse of oil, which should have lasted for only one day, burned for eight days, then day one of the eight days was natural and days two through eight were miraculous, and therefore, perhaps, the holiday should be seven days long. We might answer that the Jews' determination to even attempt to locate a cruse of kosher, pure oil was itself miraculous and worthy of celebration. The *Gemara* (Yoma 6b) points out that *halachah* does not demand that the *Menorah* be lit with pure oil at a time when the *Beit HaMikdash* and all of *Bnei Yisrael* are in a state of ritual impurity. The notion that in the filth that was the ruins of the Temple that there could even conceivably be a pure, untouched cruse of oil was ridiculous. Yet the Jews are supernatural People with supernatural expectations. That they even tried to find some pure oil was a miracle worth remembering. MRF Note: This concept of Jewish exceptionalism is reflected in Parashat Lech Lecha, when "וַיּוֹצֵא אֹתוֹ הַחוּצָה וַיֹּאמֶר הַבֶּט נָא הַשָּׁמַיְמָה וּסְפֹר הַכּוֹכָבִים אִם תּוּכַל לִסְפֹּר אֹתָם וַיֹּאמֶר לוֹ כֹּה יִהְיֶה זַרְעֶךָ," "[Hashem] took [Avram] outside, and He said, 'Please look

Heavenward and count the stars, if you are able to count them.' And He said to him, 'So will be your Seed.'" (Bereshit 15:5) Of course it is not naturally possible to count the stars. Yet that impossibility does not deter the Offspring of *Avraham Avinu*, Am *Yisrael*, from attempting to do so. And when we, like the *Chashmonaim*, attempt the impossible, *Hashem* provides a miracle and we are successful.

PURIM

5757

In the *Purim* story, each Jew gave a half *shekel* to outweigh *Haman's* bribe of 10,000 *kikar* of silver to *Achashveirosh* to kill all the Jews. "וַיֹּאמֶר הָמָן לַמֶּלֶךְ אֲחַשְׁוֵרוֹשׁ יֶשְׁנוֹ עַם אֶחָד מְפֻזָּר וּמְפֹרָד בֵּין הָעַמִּים בְּכֹל מְדִינוֹת מַלְכוּתֶךָ וְדָתֵיהֶם שֹׁנוֹת מִכָּל עָם וְאֶת דָּתֵי הַמֶּלֶךְ אֵינָם עֹשִׂים וְלַמֶּלֶךְ אֵין שֹׁוֶה לְהַנִּיחָם," "And Haman said to King Achashveirosh, 'There is a certain people <u>scattered and separate</u> among the peoples throughout all the provinces of your kingdom, and their laws differ from other peoples, and they do not keep the king's laws; it is of no use for the king to let them be." (Esther 3:8) The Jews were therefore commanded to give a half *shekel* to display our understanding of the importance of Jewish unity: that we are each only a part of the bigger picture, and without a community, we can never reach a state of completeness.

5758

Why is the book describing the amazing *Purim* story called *Megillat Esther*, rather than having been named for *Mordechai*, the other central Jewish character? One answer is that *Esther*, unlike *Mordechai*, was never in danger for her life, for it was not publicly known that she was a Jew. Yet despite her comparative safety, she risked her life for those of the Jewish People who were in danger. Furthermore, the name "Esther" comes from the root "astir," meaning "hidden." *Hashem's* Name is not mentioned any place in *Megillat Esther*, despite the fact that He is orchestrating the miraculous Jewish salvation.

The pasuk from Megillat Esther tells us that following their decisive victory, "לַיְּהוּדִים הָיְתָה אוֹרָה וְשִׂמְחָה וְשָׂשֹׂן וִיקָר," "for the Jews there were light, and happiness, and joy, and splendor." (Esther 8:16) The *Gemara* (Megillah 16b) tells us that these words respectively refer to *Torah, Yom Tov, brit milah* and *Tefillin*.

Haman believed that when his lottery to determine an auspicious date to kill the Jews resulted in the month of *Adar* (Esther 3:7), it was a good sign, since he was aware that *Moshe Rabbeinu* died on 7 *Adar*. Yet *Haman* was unaware that *Moshe* was also born on that same day, which gave the Jews a special *zechut* for survival. (Megillah 13b) The proof is provided in the *Gemara* (Kiddushin 38a). *Bnei Yisrael* cried for *Moshe* on the Plains of *Moav* for thirty days following his death (Devarim 34:8), after which *Hashem* instructed *Yehoshua* "in another three days you will be crossing this *Yarden*." (Yehoshua 1:11) Rashi calculates that this is a total of thirty-three days preceding the crossing, which we know was on 10 *Nissan*. (Yehoshua 4:19) Thirty-three days preceding 10 *Nissan* is 7 *Adar* (10 days of Nissan and 23 days of Adar), the date of *Moshe's* death. It is clear that *Moshe* was also born on 7 *Adar* because on the day of his death he states in Parashat Vayailech "ben meiah v'esrim shana anochee hayom . . . ," "I am 120 years old today," (Devarim 31:2), and Rashi confirms that this was his birthday, quoting the *Gemara* (Sotah 13b) which tells us that the *Torah* uses the word "today" to demonstrate that *Hashem* fills the days of years of the righteous to ensure they die on the very day of their birth.

5759

The *Mishnah* states "הקורא את המגילה למפרע לא יצא," "One who reads the Megillah *l'mafrayah* has not fulfilled his obligation." (Megillat 17a) "L'mafrayah" can be translated as "out of sequence," or as "retroactively," meaning applying only to the past. The *Purim* story took place in the year 3405 (corresponding to 356 BCE), in the time between the First and Second Holy Temples. The *Mishnah*, however, adjures us not to view the *Megillah* merely as an historical description of past events, but rather a narrative of the salvation of the Jewish People which has relevance to our lives today.

The *Purim Megillah* mentions the hanging death of the ten sons of Haman. (Esther 9:7-10) Curiously, within the names of the wicked sons, there is a letter "vav" written larger than all others, and there are three letters written smaller than the others: a "tav," a "shin" and a "zayin." The Hebrew letter "ו" has a *gematria* of six and "תשז" have a gematria of 707. The Hebrew year of the sixth millennium, in the year 707 (i.e. Hebrew year 5707) corresponded to the Gregorian year of 1946 CE. In fact, on October 1, 1946, which was 6 Tishrei 5707, the Nuremberg Military Tribunal tried <u>ten</u> Nazis (*yemach shemam*) and sentenced them to death by <u>hanging</u> for their modern-day "Haman-ism." Press reports from the executions report that one of them, the notorious Julius Streicher (*yemach shemo*), even cried out "Purim-Fest 1946" as his cryptic last words (despite the fact that *Purim* was more than four months in the future).

5760

The *halachah* dictates that when there are two months of *Adar* in any given calendar year (which happens seven times in nineteen years), then *Purim* is observed only once, on the Fourteenth of *Adar Sheni* (birthdays and *yahrzeits* are observed twice, in both months). *Chazal* (Megillat 6b) tell us that *Purim* must be observed in the Second *Adar* in order to connect it temporally to *Pesach*, since both holidays are rooted in the theme of *geulah*.

Rabbi Yosef Kalatsky – *Esther*, like her relative *Mordechai*, was from the Tribe of *Binyamin* (Esther 2:5-7), who was one of the two sons of *Rachel*. Haman, of course, was a direct descendant of Amalek. (Esther 3:1; I Shmuel 15:8) Our Sages state that the descendants of *Rachel* are uniquely positioned and qualified to wage war with *Amalek*. This is based on *Rachel's* understanding of how to transcend the physical/material aspects of the world. *Rachel* (like her notable descendants *Yosef* and *Esther*) was of unparalleled beauty. Despite this physical characteristic, *Rachel* successfully subdued her physical aspects for spiritual elevation and that skill/*middah* is the only remedy for combating *Amalek*, a people solely focused on the physical and entirely uninterested in the spiritual, G-dly pursuits. On *Shabbat Zachor* we are commanded to remember that *Amalek* attacked the weak of Bnei Yisrael and "he did not fear G-d." (Devarim 25:18) *Amalek* made an assessment based on purely physical criteria: the weak and old of *Bnei Yisrael* were worth attacking, but the strong and young were to be avoided. Such a people are like the thief who steals in the nighttime when no one will see or know. They fear people but not an all-seeing Creator.

Their perspective is materiality and physicality. *Rachel*, *Yosef* and *Esther* come to show us that physicality is an illusion: that true *emet* lies in *Avodat Hashem*, and with that approach, *Amalek* can be defeated.

Hamentaschen are three-sided cookies traditionally served on *Purim*. The root "tash," means "weakened." The three sides represent the Three Patriarchs who argue on behalf of the Jewish People and thereby weaken the power of *Haman* (and *Amalek*) in the world.

5761

The *Gemara* (Megillat 12a) informs us that the students of *Rabbi Shimon Bar Yochai* said that the generation of *Esther* was worthy of death not because they made use of the stolen vessels of the *Beit HaMikdash* at the *seudah* of *Achashveirosh*, but rather because they took pleasure in doing so, actually celebrating the fact that they were not redeemed and returned to *Eretz Yisrael*. MRF Note – Similarly, the *pasuk* informs us that curses shall come upon *Bnei Yisrael* "תַּחַת אֲשֶׁר לֹא עָבַדְתָּ אֶת הי אלקיך בְּשִׂמְחָה וּבְטוּב לֵבָב מֵרֹב כֹּל," "because you did not serve Hashem your G-d amid gladness and goodness of heart, when everything was abundant." (Devarim 28:47) Iturei Torah states that this is understood by the Kotzker Rebbe to mean that it was not that *Bnei Yisrael* failed to imbue their *Avodat Hashem* with *simchah* that resulted in Hashem punishing them, but rather than their failure to serve Hashem was itself imbued with *simchah*, meaning they gleefully failed to serve *Hashem* – their shortfall in serving Him was, for them, a cause for celebration, not shame.

The *Hashgachah Pratit* of *Hashem* is evident throughout the *Purim* story. In response to *Vashti's* recalcitrance and at the urging of his trusted advisors, including *Haman* (Megillah 12b), *Achashveirosh* took a rather questionable action. "וַיִּשְׁלַח סְפָרִים אֶל כָּל מְדִינוֹת הַמֶּלֶךְ אֶל מְדִינָה וּמְדִינָה כִּכְתָבָהּ וְאֶל עַם וָעָם כִּלְשׁוֹנוֹ לִהְיוֹת כָּל אִישׁ שֹׂרֵר בְּבֵיתוֹ וּמְדַבֵּר כִּלְשׁוֹן עַמּוֹ," "And he sent letters to all the king's provinces, to every province according to its writing, and to every nationality according to its language, that every man rule in his household and speak according to the language of his nationality." (Esther 1:22) The *Talmud* (Megillah 12b) tells us the patent ridiculousness of the edict created a confusion amongst the populace that caused them to hesitate when they received the subsequent decree to exterminate the Jews in a year's time. (Esther 3:13) Rather than immediately acting against the Jews, they decided to wait to determine the fallout from the edict, which gave the Jews time to engage in *teshuvah* and plan to foil *Haman's* evil plot.

5762

Rabbi Yosef Kalatsky – One may wonder why it is that, as the *Gemara* (Taanit 29a) tells us, "משנכנס אדר מרבין בשמחה," "When Adar arrives we increase in happiness." One answer is that on *Purim*, the essence of the month of *Adar*, we realize that *Hashem* saved the Jewish People despite their failings. For example, Me'Am Loez (citing *sefer* Kol Rinah) describes how some Jews participated in the decadent feast of *Achashveirosh* despite the protests and warnings from *Mordechai*. Furthermore, the *pasuk* from the *Megillah* tells us that, upon the death of *Haman*, "לַיְּהוּדִים הָיְתָה אוֹרָה וְשִׂמְחָה וְשָׂשׂן וִיקָר," "The Jews had light and joy, and gladness and honor," (Esther 8:16) and the *Gemara* (Megillah 16b) clarifies that "light" signifies *Torah*, "happiness" signifies *Yom Tovim*, "joy" signifies *brit milah* and "honor" signifies *tefillin*. This suggests that the Jews reacquired the merit of these essential mitzvot only <u>after</u> the Purim story but not <u>before</u> or <u>during</u>, which means that *Hashem* was overlooking our shortcomings in delivering our salvation. This can be distinguished from *Yom Kippur*, which the Zohar (Tikunei Zohar 57b) points out is a day "ki-purim," "like Purim," but different than *Purim*. On *Yom Kippur*, unlike on *Purim*, to achieve salvation we must own up to our failings and resolve to correct them in order to achieve atonement. No such requirement exists on *Purim*, and for that we are very happy.

Rabbi Eli Mansour – The Malbim makes a keen insight from the *Gemara* (Chulin 139b) which questions where the name "Haman" can be found in the Torah, and answers in the *pasuk* "וַיֹּאמֶר מִי הִגִּיד לְךָ כִּי עֵירֹם אָתָּה הֲמִן הָעֵץ אֲשֶׁר צִוִּיתִיךָ לְבִלְתִּי אֲכָל מִמֶּנּוּ אָכָלְתָּ," "And [Hashem] said, 'Who told you that you are naked? Have you eaten from the type of tree of which I commanded you not to eat?'" (Bereshit 3:11) The word המן here is referring to the Tree of Knowledge of Good and Evil, which *Adam* and *Chavah* were commanded not to eat. (Bereshit 2:17) They had access to all the other trees of *Gan Ayden* but could not abstain from the only one forbidden to them. So too was *Haman* obsessed with *Mordechai's* refusal to bow down to him, despite the fact that he controlled all the other Jews in his dominion. As with *Adam* and *Chavah*, *Haman's* unhealthy preoccupation with the one prohibited part of his life led to his ultimate downfall.

Chasam Sofer – Why do we celebrate *Purim* on 14 *Adar* when the miraculous military victory actually took place on 13 *Adar*, the day before? The Fourteenth Day of *Adar* was a huge celebration for the Jews, so are we not, in fact, celebrating the celebration rather than the victory over *Amalek*? One answer might be that a true victory over *Amalek* is completed only when we achieve *shalom* and *shalvah* in our lives, going about our business and living in peace without fear of *Amalek* and his genocidal plans. We conquered *Amalek* physically on 13 *Adar* but we conquered him psychologically, and therefore entirely, on 14 *Adar*, and for that we are able celebrate. The word "Amalek" has the same *gematria* as the word "safek," or "doubt." *Amalek* seeks to sow unrest through doubt in the mind of the Jew, and foiling his plan by achieving total peace of mind brings the ultimate triumph and celebration.

Rabbi Yosef Kalatsky – The *Gemara* (Megillah 7b) states the obligation that one become intoxicated on *Purim* to the point where he can no longer distinguish between the phrases "cursed is Haman" and "blessed is Mordechai." This cannot be read to encourage the confusion of the phrases or to suggest, G-d forbid, "cursed is Mordechai" or "blessed is Haman." Rather, by declaring "Blessed is Mordechai" we are, in fact, simultaneously declaring "cursed is Haman!" By making an unqualified declaration as to the value of righteousness, as embodied by *Mordechai*, we are, by implication, declaring evil, as embodied by *Haman*, as absolutely wrong. In reality, therefore, there is no difference between the two phrases, they are essentially one phrase. *Haman* only deserves to be cursed because there is a *Mordechai* who deserves to be blessed.

5763

Rabbi Moshe Weinberger – The *yetzer hara* attacks one's intellect, seemingly a Jew's most potent weapon. *Amalek*, which is *gematria* "*safek*," is the personification of the *yetzer hara*. On *Purim* we are commanded to defeat *Haman*, *Amalek*, the *yetzer hara* and all doubt. We accomplish this victory by imbibing wine for the purpose of removing mental distinctions between what is known and what is doubted or confused, thereby refusing to fight *Amalek* on his terms. Instead we pour out our love for *Hashem* through thoughtless foolishness. This duality is reflected in the *Torah* narrative about the original war between *Bnei Yisrael* and *Amalek* (Shemot 17:8-16), where when *Moshe* would hold his hand (representing deed) higher than his head (representing thought), the Jews would prevail over *Amalek*.

5764

Rabbi Eli Mansour – The happenings in the *Purim* story are otherwise very natural and understandable, yet come together for a miraculous result. This is the way by which *Hashem* manifests His Presence in the world today, which is reflected in the *modim* portion of the *Shemoneh Esrei* where we can give thanks "וְעַל נִסֶּיךָ שֶׁבְּכָל יוֹם עִמָּנוּ," "for Your miracles [provided] for us every day!"

5765

Reb Ricky Turetsky – The *Gemara* (Chulin 139b) famously informs us that *Haman* is referenced in the *Torah* when *Hashem* asks *Adam* about his having taken from the fruit of the prohibited tree. (Bereshit 3:11) Like *Adam*, who became fixated on what he could not have, *Haman* became fixated on *Mordechai*, who refused to bow down to *Haman*. Rabbi Yochanan Zweig adds that it is not merely that *Mordechai* - the <u>individual</u> - would not acknowledge *Haman*, but that *Mordechai* - the <u>Jew</u> - refused. Gentiles, even the wicked among them, have an innate understanding that the Jews are a unique and chosen People, and they therefore seek our approval and recognition based on this special status.

5766

Rabbi Michael Jablinowitz — Most years, Jews worldwide celebrate *Purim* on 14 *Adar* while the inhabitants of *Yerushalayim* observe all the *mitzvot* of *Purim* on *Shushan Purim*, the following day, on 15 *Adar*. This is because the military victory over *Haman*, the Amalekite, in *Shushan HaBirah* occurred the day after the victory was won in the rest of the empire. The *Torah* portion read on *Purim* includes the *pasuk* connecting fighting *Amalek* to the idea of "tomorrow." "וַיֹּאמֶר מֹשֶׁה אֶל-יְהוֹשֻׁעַ בְּחַר-לָנוּ אֲנָשִׁים, וְצֵא הִלָּחֵם בַּעֲמָלֵק; מָחָר, אָנֹכִי נִצָּב עַל-רֹאשׁ הַגִּבְעָה, וּמַטֵּה אלקים, בְּיָדִי," "And Moshe said to Yehoshua, 'Choose men for us, and go out and fight against Amalek. <u>Tomorrow</u> I will stand on top of the hill with the staff of G-d in my hand.'" (Shemot 17:9) The *Megillah* contains a more enigmatic reference which connects the fight and *Shushan* itself to the next day. Despite having defeated their enemies in *Shushan*, the *Megillah* tells us "וַתֹּאמֶר אֶסְתֵּר אִם עַל הַמֶּלֶךְ טוֹב יִנָּתֵן גַּם מָחָר לַיְּהוּדִים אֲשֶׁר בְּשׁוּשָׁן לַעֲשׂוֹת כְּדָת הַיּוֹם וְאֵת עֲשֶׂרֶת בְּנֵי הָמָן יִתְלוּ עַל הָעֵץ," "And Esther said, 'If it pleases the king, let <u>tomorrow</u> too be granted to the Jews to do as today's decree, and let them hang Haman's ten sons on the gallows.'" (Esther 8:13) *Shushan* was, at that time, a walled city, and therefore walled cities have a special privilege and obligation to recall the *Shushan* victory by postponing their *Purim* celebrations one day. Yet the measurement of whether or not a city is considered "walled" for these purposes is based on the city's status at the time of *Yehoshua*, not, as we would suspect, *Esther*. The *Talmud Yerushalmi* (Megillah 1b) tells us this is solely for the honor of *Yerushalayim*, which was walled when *Yehoshua* conquered

Eretz Yisrael but desolate later in the time of *Esther*. This special status is accentuated in years when *Purim* falls out on a Friday, most Jews are forced to curtail their *Purim* celebration by finishing their Purim *seudah* well before *Shabbat* (so as not to reduce the honor of *Shabbat* by failing to have a hearty appetite Friday night). In *Yerushalayim*, however, such a scenario triggers a "Purim M'Shulash," a "three-day Purim," whereby on Friday the *Megillah* is read and *matanot l'evyonim* are distributed, on *Shabbat Al HaNisim* is recited and the *parashah* of *Amalek* is read, and on Sunday there is feasting and *mishloach manot*. *Yerushalayim* had to be included in the elevated status of *Shushan Purim* cities because its ultimate glory is still to come "tomorrow." Jewish life, the Holiday of *Purim* and the City of *Yerushalayim* are collectively about optimism for the future, when the battle over *Amalek* will be won once and for all.

5767

Rabbi Yossi Jankovits – The entire Jewish People were saved in the time of *Esther* because they did not engage in *lashon hara*. Specifically, it must have been well-known that *Esther* was a Jew, as *Mordechai* had raised *Esther* in his house (Esther 2:7) and perhaps had married her (Rashi on Esther 2:7), yet neither *Achashveirosh* nor *Haman* ever knew this information until the opportune time.

5768

Rabbi Edward Davis – The *mitzvah* (Megillah 7b) of *Purim* to drink wine "ad d'lo yada bein arur Haman l'baruch Mordechai," "until one cannot distinguish between 'cursed is Haman' and 'blessed is Mordechai,'" may be an insight into the secret of Jewish salvation. Both the downfall of the wicked and the elevation of the righteous are required. We see in the *Megillah* that *Haman* was killed eleven months before the war of liberation of the Jews, as his death was a precondition to the victory. There is no distinction, or supremacy, concerning these two components, they are each equally necessary to bring about *yeshuah*.

5769

Reb Ephraim Sobol – The *Megillah* relates that *Mordechai's* revelation of the homicidal plot of *Bigtan* and *Teresh* against King *Achashveirosh* was recorded "b'Sefer Divrai Hayamim," "in the Book of the Words of Days," (Esther 2:23) the official chronicles of the kingdom. The Malbim notes that *Haman* achieved his prestige and standing in the court of King *Achashveirosh* based on having falsely replaced his name where *Mordechai's* had been recorded. Later, on the night that *Achashveirosh* was miraculously unable to sleep, the king ordered he be brought "Sefer Zichronot Divrai Hayamim," "the Book of Remembrance of the Words of Days," (Esther 6:1) which was his personal, unofficial diary. From there *Achashveirosh* learned that it was actually *Mordechai* and not *Haman* who had saved his life and thereafter grandly rewarded him. (Esther 6:10) *Achashveirosh* had been fooled by the surreptitious name substitution and was confused by the fact that it was *Esther* who had originally reported the incident to the king, (Esther 2:22) and *Esther* was queen only by virtue of *Haman's* suggestion to replace Queen *Vashti*. (Esther 1:16-19; Megillah 12b). For these reasons he originally and erroneously remembered and elevated *Haman*.

5770

Rabbi Yossi Jankovits – Why is the *Yom Tov* of *Purim* called "Purim," "lotteries?" Other *Yom Tovim* have names reflecting an essential and positive part of the historical context. For example "Chanukah" means "dedication," which refers to the successful rededication of the *Beit HaMikdash* following the military victory. "Pesach" means "pass-over," an allusion to the fact that *Hashem* Himself avoided the homes of *Bnei Yisrael* when He slew the firstborn of *Mitzrayim*. Should *Purim* have been more aptly named "Esther" or "Mordechai" in recognition of the story's heroic protagonists, rather than after the obscure and seemingly negative reference to *Haman's* infamous lottery, which he employed to pick a date on which to annihilate the Jews, G-d forbid? (Esther 3:7) The Bnei Yissaschar (Maamar Chodesh Adar 4) states that, in fact, *Purim* is an appropriate name. The Jews of the time of the *Purim* story were not deserving of salvation, as they were steeped in assimilation. By rational analysis, *Hashem* should not have intervened on their behalf. But *Haman* invoked a *pur*, which is a pure display of *Hashem's* Will to the exclusion of all human thought and analysis. *Haman* "allowed" *Hashem*, as it were, to intervene despite the fact that He had no reason to do so. Rabbi Jankovits adds that, in fact, this is why the *chukim* are a *chesed* from *Hashem* for the Jews. Rather than being a liability because we don't understand, for example, the reason for *kashrut*, these "super-rationale" *mitzvot* allow us to serve *Hashem* beyond reason. In such circumstances, as with the *Purim* lottery, *Hashem* is Willing to act *middah keneged middah* and provide *Bnei Yisrael* with *berachot* and *yeshuot* despite our not deserving them! MRF Note – Perhaps this is the deeper meaning contained in the *pasuk* from *Shacharit davening* "בַּעֲבוּר אֲבוֹתֵינוּ שֶׁבָּטְחוּ בְךָ. וַתְּלַמְּדֵם חֻקֵּי חַיִּים כֵּן תְּחָנֵּנוּ וּתְלַמְּדֵנוּ," "For the sake of our Fathers, who trusted You [Hashem], and to whom You taught the <u>enigmatic decrees of life</u>, may You supplicate and teach us as well." (הברכות שלפני קריאת שמע)

5771

MRF Note – Many reasons are given for why we do not recite *Hallel* on *Purim*. The *Gemara* (Megillah 14a) cites *Rav Nachman's* position that reading the *Megillah* is equivalent to reciting *Hallel*. *Hallel* itself has two major themes: requests to *Hashem* on one hand (e.g. "אנא הי הושיעה נא," "Please, Hashem, save now!"), and praise and thanksgiving on the other (e.g. "הוֹדוּ לַיי כִּי טוֹב כִּי לְעוֹלָם חַסְדוֹ," "Give thanks to Hashem, for He is Good, His Kindness endures forever!"). The *Gemara* (Megillah 4a) also tells us that *Rabbi Yehoshua ben Levy* says that a person is obligated to read *Megillat Esther* on both the night and day of *Purim*. In support of this requirement he cites the *pasuk* "אלקי אֶקְרָא יוֹמָם וְלֹא תַעֲנֶה וְלַיְלָה וְלֹא דוּמִיָּה לִי," "My G-d, I <u>call out</u> by day and You do not reply, and by night, and I have no respite," (Tehillim 22:3) which demonstrates the aspect of petitioning *Hashem*. Significantly, also in support of the night and day obligation to read, the same *Gemara* cites *Rabi Chelbo* who quotes the *pasuk* "לְמַעַן | יְזַמֶּרְךָ כָבוֹד

וְלֹא יִדֹּם הִי אלקי לְעוֹלָם אוֹדֶךָּ," "So that my soul will sing praises to You and not be silent. Hashem, G-d, forever I will thank You," (Tehillim 30:13) which demonstrates the aspect of praise and thanksgiving. We see that the two *pasukim* the *Gemara* cites for the double recitation of the *Megillah* are themselves demonstrative of the dual aspects of *Hallel*, which might help us understand better why the *Megillah* can be a substitute for *Hallel* on the Holiday of *Purim*.

5772

Reb Moshe Feiglin – There are alarming parallels between the conduct of *King Achashveirosh* with respect to *Queen Vashti* and Israeli Prime Minister Ariel Sharon and his treatment of the Jews of *Gush Katif*. The *Gemara* (Megillah 12b) relates that the king demanded that his wife appear before the revelers of his feast in nothing but her crown, a patently immoral order. When she refused, the king sought counsel as to what "כְּדָת מַה לַּעֲשׂוֹת בַּמַּלְכָּה וַשְׁתִּי עַל | אֲשֶׁר לֹא עָשְׂתָה אֶת מַאֲמַר הַמֶּלֶךְ אֲחַשְׁוֵרוֹשׁ בְּיַד הַסָּרִיסִים," "according to the law, could be done to Queen Vashti, as she had not complied with the order of King Achashveirosh, by the hand of the deputies." (Esther 1:15) For his "legal" determination as to whether or not to eliminate her, "וַיֹּאמֶר הַמֶּלֶךְ לַחֲכָמִים יֹדְעֵי הָעִתִּים כִּי כֵן דְּבַר הַמֶּלֶךְ לִפְנֵי כָּל יֹדְעֵי דָּת וָדִין," "the king then spoke to his wise advisors who understood the times, for this was the way of the king to seek those who know law and judgment." (Esther 1:13) His advisors cautioned him about the "slippery slope" of spousal insubordination that would ensue throughout all the king's provinces if *Vashti's* defiance went unchecked, which would ultimately delegitimize the king's power. (Esther 1:17, 18) This gave *Achashveirosh* the legal and political cover to have her killed, with the power of the state behind him. Following the events of the *Purim* story, his kingdom was soon ended, as such an abuse of power is always the ultimate undoing of a tyrant. Sharon used the power of the state to immorally destroy *Gush Katif*, invoking in the process that notion that legal orders needed to be followed for the good of the state. His political party, created for the sole purpose of pushing through the expulsion, has since all but disappeared, while the whole Gaza "disengagement" is now broadly recognized as an unnecessary disaster.

5773

Rabbi Eli Mansour – *Haman* is from *Amalek*. (Esther 3:1) "וַיָּבֹא עֲמָלֵק וַיִּלָּחֶם עִם יִשְׂרָאֵל בִּרְפִידִם," "Amalek came and battled Yisrael at Refidim." (Shemot 17:8) The Midrash Tanchuma (25) states that "refidim" is a contraction of "refu yadam," "weakened hands," meaning because the Jews became lax in Torah study (of what had been learned at *Marah* (Shemot 15:25), *Amalek* attacked. The implication is that diligent and continuous *Torah* study is the best preventive measure against *Amalek*, both in his external form and his internal manifestation as the *yetzer hara*.

PESACH

5757

In *Kiddush* for both *Shabbat* and *Yom Tov* we recite the "zacheir l'tziat Mitzrayim," which literally translates as "a remembrance of the Exodus of Egypt," rather than "a remembrance of the Exodus from Egypt." It is not so much that *Bnei Yisrael* left Egypt but that the negative spiritual essence of Egypt left *Bnei Yisrael* when the Ten Plagues made us a Nation.

5758

Eliyahu HaNavi is at every circumcision at *Hashem's* command. (Pirkei d'Rabbi Eliezer 29) He is therefore at every *Seder*, where Jewish law dictates that one may not participate unless one is circumcised. (Shemot 12:48)

5759

The number four is very prominent at the *Pesach Seder*. Four cups (representing the *Arba'ah Leshonot Geulah*), four questions, and four sons. There is a *pasuk* that reads "שְׁמַע בְּנִי מוּסַר אָבִיךָ וְאַל תִּטֹּשׁ תּוֹרַת אִמֶּךָ," "Hearken, my son, to the discipline of your father, and do not forsake the instruction of your mother." (Mishlei 1:8) One works to acquire his father's values (they are not innate), but one works to retain his mother's values (which are innate). The law of the mother is minimal Judaism, yet is essential to Jewish survival. It forms the basis of the Jewish Nation. "אומה," "nation" has the same *shoresh* as "אמא," "mother." There are four "mothers" of the Jewish Nation, *Sarah*, *Rivkah*, *Rachel* and *Leah*, and their imprint of "four" is prominent at *Pesach*, the time when the irreducible common National bond is highlighted (e.g. with the four sons of varying religious connection).

The wise son asks an enigmatic question: "חָכָם מָה הוּא אוֹמֵר? מָה הָעֵדוֹת וְהַחֻקִּים וְהַמִּשְׁפָּטִים אֲשֶׁר צִוָּה ה' אֱלֹקֵינוּ אֶתְכֶם. וְאַף אַתָּה אֱמֹר לוֹ כְּהִלְכוֹת הַפֶּסַח: אֵין מַפְטִירִין אַחַר הַפֶּסַח אֲפִיקוֹמָן," "What does the wise [son] say? 'What are these testimonies, statutes and judgments that Hashem our G-d commanded you?' And accordingly you will say to him, 'as per the laws of the Pesach [sacrifice], we may not eat an Afikoman after the Pesach [sacrifice].'" In essence he is inquiring as to the legal basis for eating *matzah* on the *Seder* night (15 Nissan) before we eat the *Afikoman*, which represents the *Korban Pesach*, which we originally designated earlier (10 Nissan) in Egypt. His question is strengthened based on the *halachah* that an animal korban (which the *Afikoman* represents) takes precedence over a meal offering (represented by *matzah*). We answer the *chacham* that the particular law of the *Seder* is that, according to Shulchan Aruch (Orach Chayim 478:1), the *Afikoman* is the last item we may eat, but we indicate that both his question and his proofs are legitimate.

There are many interpretations of what *chametz* represents and why, therefore, it is proscribed on *Pesach*. (1) *avodah zareh* – *Bnei Yisrael* took a *Korban Pesach* in *Mitzrayim* because the lamb was worshipped by the Egyptians. (Rashi on Shemot 12:6) The Zohar (2:182) says that one who eats *chametz* on *Pesach* is like an idolator. The Rambam says that there is a prohibition of *chametz* on the *Mizbeach* because of the prevailing historical practice of idolators to serve their gods using *chametz*. During *Pesach* we are forbidden to even see *chametz*. We must burn it, eradicate its existence, and we cannot benefit from it in any way. This "zero tolerance" standard is identical to the *halachic* standard for *avodah zareh*. (2) *yetzer hara* – The yeast that make dough rise is compared to the ego that leads to haughtiness, which is inconsistent with service to *Hashem*. (3) human ingenuity – The man-made manipulation of *Hashem's* world is evident in the addition of *se'or* to the bread baking process. While such manipulation is normally accepted and even encouraged, during *Pesach* we are commanded to yield to *Hashem's* supervision and resist imposing our own will. (4) completeness – *Pesach*, *Z'man Cheroteinu*, is merely a beginning of a process that leads to *Shavuot*, *Z'man Matan Torateinu*. In Temple times, this involved the daily bringing of the *Omer* offering, which now is remembered through *Sefirat HaOmer*. Since the achievement of freedom is an incomplete status until it is supplemented with the giving of the *Torah* by which to order and add meaning to our lives, we do not eat *chametz*, which represents completeness, on *Pesach*.

Seder Olam Rabbah (chapter 3) tells us that while the *shibud* of *Mitzrayim* lasted for 210 years, the period during which *Bnei Yisrael* was subjected to slave labor was eighty-six years. The period of enslavement was originally decreed to last 430 years (Shemot 12:41), which is five periods of eighty-six years each. We raise and drink a cup of wine to *Hashem* for each of the four periods of eighty-six year each that we were not forced to work. Interestingly, the *gematria* of the Hebrew word for cup, כוס, is 86!

5760

Rabbi Meir Shapiro – What is the significance of having a boiled egg on the *Seder* plate? Eggs, unlike other foods, become firmer the longer they are cooked. This is comparable to *Bnei Yisrael* in *Mitzrayim*, who multiplied under the burdens of *Paroh*. (Shemot 1:12)

Rabbi Edward Davis – There is a *minhag* among some *chassidim* who abstain from *gebrochtz* during *Pesach* to eat *gebrochtz* on the last day of the *Chag* as a show of unity with *Am Yisrael*. This displays an awareness that those who eat *gebrochtz* are not eating *chametz*, chas v'shalom. Gebrochtz is entirely permissible and while the *chassidim* are stringent they do not claim others are wrong or, G-d forbid, *treif*.

There are four expressions of *geulah* by *Hashem* as set forth in Parashat Vaeira that are the source for the four cups of wine at the *Pesach Seder*. "Hotzaiti," "I will take you out," "Hitzalti," "I will rescue you," "Gaalti," "I will redeem you," and "Lakachti," "I will take you." (Shemot 6:6, 7)

The untenable assertion that G-d is merely the Originator of Creation but is not thereafter involved in the details of the world is belied by the first of the Ten Commandments and related to the holiday of Passover, which is the identification of *Hashem* as the One who took *Bnei Yisrael* out of Egypt, and not only as the Creator of the World. The entire plague process is a study in *Hashem's* absolute control of His World and actualization of His Will to elevate the Jews and crush *Mitzrayim*. This critical realization on the part of *Bnei Yisrael* required immediate institution of a formal mechanism to retain this clarity. The *Torah* therefore gives the *mitzvot* of *Pesach* before *Matan Torah* as an "eternal decree." (Shemot 12:14) Freedom therefore came before the cessation of servitude, for it was rooted in properly understanding the Omnipotence of *Hashem*.

Rabbi Yosef Kalatsky – With regard to the first plague of blood, the *Torah* tells us that *Hashem* commanded *Moshe* "כֹּה אָמַר ה' בְּזֹאת תֵּדַע כִּי אֲנִי ה' הִנֵּה אָנֹכִי מַכֶּה | בַּמַּטֶּה אֲשֶׁר בְּיָדִי עַל הַמַּיִם אֲשֶׁר בַּיְאֹר וְנֶהֶפְכוּ לְדָם וְהַדָּגָה אֲשֶׁר בַּיְאֹר תָּמוּת וּבָאַשׁ הַיְאֹר" "So said Hashem, 'With this you will know that I am Hashem. Behold, I will smite with the staff that is in My hand upon the water that is in the river, and it will turn to blood. And the fish that are in the river will die, and the river will become putrid.'" (Shemot 7:17, 18) *Moshe* then followed *Hashem's* instructions and the Nile turned to blood, the fish died, and the stench ensued. (Shemot 7:20, 21) The *Torah* then goes on to tell us that magicians of Egypt "vayaasu khain," "did the same." (Shemot 7:22) The Sforno points out that they really did not do the same thing. Their witchcraft turned water (purchased from Jews) into red water with the appearance of blood, but it was not turned to actual blood, a fundamental change in nature of which only *Hashem* is capable. No fish died in the magician's trick, which in the case of the Nile was the true proof that the water had been transformed into blood. Yet the following *pasuk* tells us "וַיִּפֶן פַּרְעֹה וַיָּבֹא אֶל בֵּיתוֹ וְלֹא שָׁת לִבּוֹ גַּם לָזֹאת" "Paroh turned and went home, and he paid no heed even to this." (Shemot 7:23) It was enough for him that his magicians had come close to duplicating the plague. Any excuse was required to avoid the truth of *Hashem's* Omnipotence. We, in this way, are much like *Paroh*. We look for refutation of fundamental truths. These refutations are clearly not *emet* but are <u>some</u> evidence by which to avoid our obligations. We then return to our "ivory towers," avoiding personal growth and commitment, until, of course, *Hashem* gives us *emet* we cannot avoid, but which is more painful. MRF Note – This may be reflected in the phenomenon of Jews who scour the secular press for the occasional story of a religious Jew who exhibited unethical public behavior, and then use such an example as a justification not to adopt a *Torah* lifestyle themselves.

5761

Rabbi Yossi Jankovits – In our times, without a *Beit HaMikdash*, eating *matzah* is a positive *mitzvah* for the first night of *Pesach* only. (Shulchan Aruch O.C. 475:7) The *Torah* does state "בָּרִאשֹׁן בְּאַרְבָּעָה עָשָׂר יוֹם לַחֹדֶשׁ בָּעֶרֶב תֹּאכְלוּ מַצֹּת עַד יוֹם הָאֶחָד וְעֶשְׂרִים לַחֹדֶשׁ בָּעֶרֶב," "In the first [month], on the fourteenth day of the month in the evening, you shall eat matzot, until the twenty first day of the month in the evening." (Shemot 12:18) An earlier *pasuk*, however, states "וְאָכְלוּ אֶת הַבָּשָׂר בַּלַּיְלָה הַזֶּה צְלִי אֵשׁ וּמַצּוֹת עַל מְרֹרִים יֹאכְלֻהוּ", "and they shall eat the meat on this night, roasted over the fire, and matzot; with maror they shall eat it" (Shemot 12:8), indicating that eating *matzah* is connected to the eating of the *Korban Pesach*, which we cannot currently bring, along with *maror*. The *Torah* does mention that one must eat *matzah* for seven days when describing the requirement of removing all *chametz*, which is viewed as a sign of haughtiness, from one's home (Shemot 12:15), but the Sages understood that because there is both a positive command and a separate negative command, one need not eat *matzah* on *Pesach* after the first day, and certainly need not eat *shmurah matzah*.

The fixed construction of the modern Hebrew calendar dictates that the first day of *Pesach* cannot be Monday, Wednesday or Friday, which means the first *Seder* cannot be Sunday night, Tuesday night or Thursday night. This is because the calendar also demands that the day upon which each day of *Pesach* falls must also be the day of a corresponding Jewish holiday. Specifically:

First day of Pesach – *Tisha B'Av*
Second day of Pesach – First day of *Shavuot*; *Hoshana Rabbah*
Third day of Pesach – *Rosh Hashanah*; First day of *Sukkot*; and *Shemini Atzeret*
Fourth day of Pesach – *Simchat Torah*
Fifth day of Pesach – *Yom Kippur*
Sixth day of Pesach – *Lag B'Omer*

Based on this structure, if the first day of *Pesach* were to fall on a Monday, then the fifth day of *Pesach* would fall on a Friday, which would mean *Yom Kippur* would be on Friday. That would be untenable, for *Yom Kippur* itself is called "Shabbat Shabbaton," "Sabbath of all Sabbaths" (Vayikra 23:32), which means it is a *Yom Tov* treated like *Shabbat* by *halachah*. Because we are obligated in Tosefet Shabbat (Rosh Hashanah 9a), it would be incompatible to have one "Shabbat" (i.e. *Yom Kippur*) run into another one (i.e. *Shabbat*). For the same reason, the first day of *Pesach* cannot fall on Wednesday, because the fifth day of *Pesach* would be Sunday, which would mean *Yom Kippur* would be on Sunday, making it irreconcilably adjacent to *Shabbat*. Finally, if the first day of *Pesach* were to fall on Friday, then the second day of *Pesach* would be on *Shabbat*, and *Hoshana Rabbah* would likewise fall on *Shabbat*. *Chazal* prohibited this outcome to ensure that *Klal Yisrael* could take the *aravot* on *Hoshana Rabbah*.

Rabbi Yisroel Ciner – In *Sefer* Daniel the wicked king *Nevuchadnezair* decreed "וּמַן דִּי לָא יִפֵּל וְיִסְגֻּד יִתְרְמֵא לְגוֹא אַתּוּן נוּרָא יָקִדְתָּא" "And whoever does not fall and prostrate himself [in idol worship] shall be cast into the fiery furnace." (Daniel 3:11) His three Jewish advisors *Chananyah*, *Misha'el* and *Azaryah* refused, and opted to be thrown into an oven to sanctify G-d's name. From where did they learn that this was proper conduct? The *Talmud* (Pesachim 53b) states that they learned it from the Plague of Frogs. When *Moshe* warned *Paroh* about the impending plague he said "וְשָׁרַץ הַיְאֹר צְפַרְדְּעִים וְעָלוּ וּבָאוּ בְּבֵיתֶךָ וּבַחֲדַר מִשְׁכָּבְךָ וְעַל מִטָּתֶךָ וּבְבֵית עֲבָדֶיךָ וּבְעַמֶּךָ וּבְתַנּוּרֶיךָ וּבְמִשְׁאֲרוֹתֶיךָ" "And the River will swarm with frogs, and they will go up and come into your house and into your bedroom and upon your bed and into the house of your servants and into your people, and into your ovens and into your kneading troughs." (Shemot 7:28) Some frogs realized that while entering the oven would mean certain death, to not do so could raise a question concerning *Hashem's* Powers, G-d forbid. The Yalkut Shemoni (end of remez 182) states that, like *Chananyah*, *Misha'el* and *Azaryah*, the frogs that did enter the ovens survived when the plague ended.

5762

Rabbi Eli Mansour – The Malbim (Midrash Haggadah Shel Pesach) draws a comparison from the *Haggadah* between *Dayeinu* and *Nishmat Kol Chai*, which we also recite during the *Shabbat* and *Yom Tov davening*. In *Dayeinu* we are not stating, G-d forbid, that if *Hashem* had, for example, taken us out of Egypt but not given us the *Torah*, then we would have been satisfied as a Nation. Rather, we are declaring our understanding that if *Hashem* had provided for us any one of the enumerated benefits, that would have singularly been enough to require us to thank Him in an unlimited fashion of ascending praises. Indeed, in *Nishmat Kol Chai*, we affirm that even if we, as a Nation, possessed the most expansive physical and spiritual powers we could not adequately thank and praise *Hashem* for the myriad of miracles that He performs for us regularly. Then, surprisingly, we recite the following: "עַל כֵּן אֵבָרִים שֶׁפִּלַּגְתָּ בָּנוּ. וְרוּחַ וּנְשָׁמָה שֶׁנָּפַחְתָּ בְּאַפֵּינוּ. וְלָשׁוֹן אֲשֶׁר שַׂמְתָּ בְּפִינוּ. הֵן הֵם. יוֹדוּ וִיבָרְכוּ וִישַׁבְּחוּ וִיפָאֲרוּ וִירוֹמְמוּ וְיַעֲרִיצוּ וְיַקְדִּישׁוּ וְיַמְלִיכוּ אֶת שִׁמְךָ מַלְכֵּנוּ," "Therefore the organs that You placed within us and the spirit and the soul that You breathed into our nostrils, and the tongue that You placed in our mouth – all of them shall thank and bless, praise and glorify, exalt and revere, sanctify and declare the Kingship of Your Name." (Siddur) From where does *Bnei Yisrael* get the apparent *chutzpah* to, in one breath, tell *Hashem* that we lack the physical and spiritual resources to ever sufficiently thank and praise Him, and then immediately thereafter use most exalted terms to do exactly that. Rabbi Mansour brings a *mashal* to resolve the contradiction. There once was a king who asked his most trusted and loyal nobleman to host a party in his honor. When the king arrived at the party he was surprised to find the nobleman depressed, despite the festive atmosphere. To test him, the king instructed the nobleman to throw a second party in his honor the following night, and to use only $100,000 from the royal treasury for the event. Upon arriving at the second party, the king was disappointed to see the nobleman in a state of near ecstasy, clearly enjoying himself fully. The king pulled the nobleman aside and rebuked him strongly. "When you were forced to fund my party you were in despair, yet when I provided the funding your happiness knows no bounds. Explain yourself!" The nobleman then calmly replied to the king, "Your majesty, you don't understand. When you left me to my own devices, judgment and resources I was distraught, knowing full well that no matter how much I spent I could never adequately thank and honor you in proportion to what you truly deserve. Yet at the second party, when you provided a fixed amount and instructed me to do the best I could, despite the limitation, I could truly rejoice."

Reb Ricky Turetsky - In Parashat Bo, *Hashem* informs *Bnei Yisrael* that the reason for the wondrous plagues in *Mitzrayim* is "וּלְמַעַן תְּסַפֵּר בְּאָזְנֵי בִנְךָ וּבֶן בִּנְךָ אֵת אֲשֶׁר הִתְעַלַּלְתִּי בְּמִצְרַיִם וְאֶת אֹתֹתַי אֲשֶׁר שַׂמְתִּי בָם וִידַעְתֶּם כִּי אֲנִי ה'", "in order that you tell into the ears of your son and your son's son how I made sport of the Egyptians, and that you tell of My signs that I placed in them, and [then] you will know that I am Hashem." (Shemot 10:2) HaRav Yochanan Zweig states that the *lashon* of the *pasuk* tells us that one must tell the story of the Exodus into the ears of his children and his grandchildren, and "<u>then</u> you will know I am G-d." When there are three generations of *frum* Jews gathered to recount the story of the Exodus, <u>then</u> one has proof positive of *Hashem's* existence.

5763

Rabbi Yitzchak Assouli – The word "paroh" is from the Hebrew word "parua," meaning "unbridled." "Mitzrayim" is from the word "meitzar," which means "constraint" or "limitation." Rabbi Eliyahu Eliezer Dessler says that the *yetzer hara*, which is our own, personal "*Paroh*," tries to convince one that he will be "unbridled" by *mitzvot*, and when he listens, one feels free at first but soon ends up enslaved in "*Mitzrayim*," a prisoner to his desires.

Dr. David Epstein – With regard to the Exodus, the *Torah* says "וַיָּבֹאוּ בְנֵי יִשְׂרָאֵל בְּתוֹךְ הַיָּם בַּיַּבָּשָׁה וְהַמַּיִם לָהֶם חוֹמָה מִימִינָם וּמִשְּׂמֹאלָם", "Then the Children of Israel came into the midst of the sea on dry land, and the waters were to them as a wall from their right and from their left". (Shemot 14:22) The word "chomah," "wall," is spelled with a "vav." Later, the pasuk states "וּבְנֵי יִשְׂרָאֵל הָלְכוּ בַיַּבָּשָׁה בְּתוֹךְ הַיָּם וְהַמַּיִם לָהֶם חֹמָה מִימִינָם וּמִשְּׂמֹאלָם", "But the Children of Israel went on dry land in the midst of the sea, and the water was to them like a wall from their right and from their left." (Shemot

14:29) Here the same word "chomah" is missing the "vav," which allows it to be read "chamah," or "anger." The Vilna Gaon says there were two groups at *Kriyat Yam Suf*. The first group to cross (described in the first *pasuk*) went "b'toch hayam bayabashah," "into the sea; on dry land," and the other (described in the second *pasuk*) followed the first group, and went "bayabashah b'toch hayam," "on dry land; into the sea." The first group demonstrated trust that *Hashem* would save them and "got wet," while the second group waited for the first group to "blaze the trail," and then comfortably followed them "on dry land." This second approach evinced a lack of *bitachon*, and angered *Hashem*, hence the use of the word "chamah" to describe the second group. MRF Note: The difference between being "involved" and being "committed" is that, in an egg and steak breakfast, the chicken was involved, the cow was committed.

Chida – The *Haggadah* states "בָּרוּךְ הַמָּקוֹם, בָּרוּךְ הוּא, בָּרוּךְ שֶׁנָּתַן תּוֹרָה לְעַמּוֹ יִשְׂרָאֵל, בָּרוּךְ הוּא. כְּנֶגֶד אַרְבָּעָה בָנִים דִּבְּרָה תוֹרָה," "Blessed is Hashem, Blessed is He; Blessed is the One who Gave the Torah to His People Yisrael, Blessed is He. Corresponding to four sons did the Torah speak." What is the connection between the Giving of the Torah and the Four Sons? The Talmud (Shabbat 88b) relates that when the time came for *Hashem* to give *Am Yisrael* the *Torah* the *malachim* objected. Their basic argument was to invoke the *halachah* of "bar metzra," "the adjoining property holder." According to this law, as set forth in Shulchan Aruch (Choshen Mishpat 175) when an owner seeks to transfer his property he must first offer it to his immediate neighbors, who have a right of first refusal. The *malachim* argued therefore that as *Hashem's* "neighbors" in *Shamayim*, they, and not the Jews, had first rights to the *Torah*. There is, however, an exception to the basic rule of "bar metzrah," which is that the son of the owner has priority over even the immediate neighbor. The *Gemara* (Kiddushin 36a) records the debate between *Rabbi Yehudah* and *Rabbi Meir* as to whether or not *Bnei Yisrael* are considered the Children of *Hashem*, even when we sin. Although in most such debates we *poskin* the *halachah* like *Rabbi Yehudah*, on this question we hold like *Rabbi Meir*; that the Jews are always regarded like the Sons of *Hashem*. Based on this *halachah*, the Jews had priority over the *malachim* for receiving the *Torah* from *Hashem*, and this is why the Four Sons are connected in the *Haggadah* to the portion in praise to *Hashem* for giving His Children the *Torah*.

Paroh decides that the Plague of Frogs must end and summons *Moshe* to his palace. (Shemot 8:4) Suspecting that the plague will end when he cries "uncle," *Paroh* tries to outwit *Moshe* by telling him that *Hashem* should remove the plague "l'machar," "for tomorrow." (Shemot 8:6) *Paroh* was wagering that *Hashem* would end the plague immediately, which would demonstrate some sort of lacking in His Power in not waiting until the next day. This is an incredible insight into the mania of the human mind: a willingness to take a chance of enduring additional unnecessary pain in order to prove a point.

5764

Rabbi Edward Davis – The *Kos shel Eliyahu* is obviously not poured during the *Seder* to allow *Eliyahu* to drink, but rather for him to *poskin*. There is a question, based on the *Arba'ah Leshonot Geulah* (Shemot 6:6, 7), as to whether there should be four or five cups at the *Seder*. The first four expressions of redemption form the basis of the Four Cups that are universally recognized, but the fifth expression "וְהֵבֵאתִי אֶתְכֶם אֶל הָאָרֶץ אֲשֶׁר נָשָׂאתִי אֶת יָדִי לָתֵת אֹתָהּ לְאַבְרָהָם לְיִצְחָק וּלְיַעֲקֹב וְנָתַתִּי אֹתָהּ לָכֶם מוֹרָשָׁה אֲנִי הי", "I will bring you to the Land, concerning which I raised My Hand to give to Avraham, to Yitzchak, and to Yaacov, and I will give it to you as a Heritage; I am Hashem" (Shemot 6:8) is questioned. It makes no sense that *Eliyahu HaNavi* would drink wine at every *Seder*, for he would be plenty drunk if he did, but rather he comes to resolve this question that is captured by the inclusion of a fifth cup for him on the *Seder* table.

5765

Rabbi Avi Weiss – Rabbi Aaron Soloveitchik made a distinction between two terms for rescue – *hatzalah* and *yeshuah*. *Hatzalah* requires no action on the part of the person being saved, but *yeshuah* does demand that the person help himself before *Hashem* will redeem him. At the time of the Exodus, the *pasuk* states "לָכֵן אֱמֹר לִבְנֵי יִשְׂרָאֵל אֲנִי ה' וְהוֹצֵאתִי אֶתְכֶם מִתַּחַת סִבְלֹת מִצְרַיִם וְהִצַּלְתִּי אֶתְכֶם מֵעֲבֹדָתָם וְגָאַלְתִּי אֶתְכֶם בִּזְרוֹעַ נְטוּיָה וּבִשְׁפָטִים גְּדֹלִים," "Therefore, say to Bnei Yisrael, 'I am Hashem, and I will <u>save you</u> out from under the burdens of the Egyptians, and I will <u>save you</u> from their labor, and I will redeem you with an outstretched Arm and with great Judgments.'" (Shemot 6:6) Here the term *hatzalah* is used, as *Hashem* pledges to redeem the newborn and helpless *Am Yisrael*. Later, by *Kriyat Yam Suf*, the *pasuk* states "<u>וַיּוֹשַׁע</u> ה' בַּיּוֹם הַהוּא אֶת יִשְׂרָאֵל מִיַּד מִצְרָיִם וַיַּרְא יִשְׂרָאֵל אֶת מִצְרַיִם מֵת עַל שְׂפַת הַיָּם," "On that day Hashem <u>saved</u> Yisrael from the hand of the Egyptians, and Yisrael saw the Egyptians dying on the seashore." (Shemot 14:30) Here, and in other places in the *Yam Suf* narrative (e.g. Shemot 14:13), the Jews were expected by *Hashem* to have "grown-up" to some extent and to take an active role in their salvation, by, for example, entering the sea before it split. Rav Kook says this required element of redemption is manifested in our opening the door for *Eliyahu HaNavi* at the end of the *Seder*.

5766

Rabbi Michael Jablinowitz – When summoned by *Hashem* to lead the Jewish People in their *geulah* from *Mitzrayim*, "וַיְדַבֵּר מֹשֶׁה לִפְנֵי ה' לֵאמֹר הֵן בְּנֵי יִשְׂרָאֵל לֹא שָׁמְעוּ אֵלַי וְאֵיךְ יִשְׁמָעֵנִי פַרְעֹה וַאֲנִי עֲרַל שְׂפָתָיִם," "Moshe spoke before Hashem, saying, 'Behold, the Children of Israel did not hearken to me. How then will Paroh hearken to me, seeing that I am of <u>closed lips</u>." (shemot 6:12) Ultimately, *Bnei Yisrael* depart *Mitzrayim* during "Pesach," which the Kedushas Levi (Derush LePesach 61c) interprets as "Peh Sach," the "Mouth Speaks." The obvious imagery connects the importance of speech in bringing about *geulah*. We know that *lashon hara* brought about the destruction of the Second *Beit HaMikdash* (Sefer Chofetz Chaim, introduction) and keeps it from being rebuilt. We should focus on removing the *orlah* of the lips and using the tremendous power of speech to bring goodness and, ultimately, redemption to the world.

5767

Rabbeinu Bachaiya - *Hashem's* four promises, as contained in the *Arb'ah Leshonot Geulah*, the Four Expressions of Redemption (Shemot 6:6, 7), are all fulfilled over time. 1. "I shall take you out of service" – this began with the first plague of *dam*. (Shemot 7:20) 2. "I shall rescue you from service" – this was walking out of Egypt, from *Ramses* to *Sukkot*. (Shemot 12:37) 3. "I shall redeem you" – this happened at *Yam Suf*, when *Bnei Yisrael* became truly free with the drowning death of their captors. (Shemot 14:30) 4. "I shall take you as a People" – this occurred at *Matan Torah* at *Har Sinai*. (Shemot 19:6) What is not often cited is the continuation of the Four Expressions that immediately follows: "וִידַעְתֶּם כִּי אֲנִי ה' הַמּוֹצִיא אֶתְכֶם מִתַּחַת סִבְלוֹת מִצְרָיִם וְהֵבֵאתִי אֶתְכֶם אֶל הָאָרֶץ אֲשֶׁר נָשָׂאתִי אֶת יָדִי לָתֵת אֹתָהּ לְאַבְרָהָם לְיִצְחָק וּלְיַעֲקֹב וְנָתַתִּי אֹתָהּ לָכֶם מוֹרָשָׁה אֲנִי ה'" . . . <u>and you will know that I am Hashem your G-d</u>, Who has brought you out from under the burdens of Mitzrayim. I will bring you to the Land, concerning which I raised My Hand to give to Avraham, to Yitzchak, and to Yaacov, and I will give it to you as a heritage; I am Hashem." (Shemot 6:7, 8) The additional text could be read to require our recognition of *Hashem* as a condition precedent to our *Geulah*, and perhaps alludes to *Moshiach* and the time in the future at which the Jews (and all nations) will know for certain that *Hashem* is One.

5768

Reb Dani Bengio – On the seventh day of *Pesach* we celebrate the crossing of the *Yam Suf*. In *Hallel* we declare "הַיָּם רָאָה וַיָּנֹס . . . הֶהָרִים רָקְדוּ כְאֵילִים," "the sea saw . . . the mountains skipped like rams." (Tehillim 114:3, 4) The sea saw that the *Mitzrim*, having effectively violated *Bnei Yisrael*, *Hashem's* betrothed, were liable based on *halachah* for death by stoning (*skilah*), and not drowning (which is the equivalent of *chenek*, Ketubot 30a), and therefore deferred to the mountains (comprised of stone) to impose the penalty. Yet *Hashem* decreed that because the *Mitzrim* drowned the Jewish boys in the Nile (Shemot 1:22), *middah keneged middah* they themselves were destined to be drowned. Yet the Torah tells us that "וַיָּבֹאוּ בְנֵי יִשְׂרָאֵל בְּתוֹךְ הַיָּם בַּיַּבָּשָׁה וְהַמַּיִם לָהֶם חוֹמָה מִימִינָם וּמִשְּׂמֹאלָם," "Then Bnei Yisrael came into the midst of the sea on dry land, and the waters were to them as a wall to their right and to their left." (Shemot 14:22) While the Egyptians surely drowned, they were also pounded by the "walls" of water which satisfied the requirement that they be subjected to *skilah*. *Sefer* Chanukas HaTorah points out that the *Talmud* (Sanhedrin 95b) cites another potential form of execution for the *Mitzrim* was the *shirah* of the *malachim*. The *Gemara* (Megillah 10b) relays the *Midrash* that when the Egyptians were drowning in the sea, the angels wanted to say a *shirah*, but *Hashem* said to them "My creations are drowning in the sea and you would say *shirah*?" Perhaps *Hashem* was not, as is commonly understood, excoriating the angels for singing at a time when the Egyptians were being killed, but rather simply pointing out that drowning, and not *shirah*, was specifically required as the mode of their destruction.

5769

Rabbi Yosef Weinstock – The Sefas Emes notes that, following the miracle of *Kriyat Yam Suf*, the *mayim* wanted to remain split as a *Kiddush Hashem* to the world. *Hashem* therefore had to specifically command that the waters return to their fixed, natural state. The Sefas Emes understands this to explain the statement in the *Gemara* (Sotah 2a; Sanhedrin 22a) that making a proper *shidduch* is as difficult as splitting the sea. In fact, many singles believe that their *Avodat Hashem* would be enhanced if they remained a "wall" of independence, not comingled with a spouse, thereby creating a greater *Kiddush Hashem* than could be accomplished with a mate. To this *Hashem* indicates this is not what He desires, but rather that we "mix" with a life mate in a natural, but perhaps more mundane way.

Rabbi Chaim Zvi Senter – The *pasuk* states that during the Plague of the Firstborn, "וּלְכֹל בְּנֵי יִשְׂרָאֵל לֹא יֶחֱרַץ כֶּלֶב לְשֹׁנוֹ לְמֵאִישׁ וְעַד בְּהֵמָה לְמַעַן תֵּדְעוּן אֲשֶׁר יַפְלֶה הי בֵּין מִצְרַיִם וּבֵין יִשְׂרָאֵל," "But to all Bnei Yisrael, not one dog will whet its tongue against either man or beast, in order that you shall know that Hashem will separate between the Mitzrim and between Yisrael." (Shemot 11:7) The original cause of the Egyptian *galut* was the *lashon hara* of *Yosef* that generated strife with his brothers. (Bereshit 37:2) This was what prompted *Moshe* to declare "indeed, the matter is known," (Shemot 2:14), meaning the exile persists because of the *lashon hara* that *Datan* and *Aviram* spoke about *Moshe* to *Paroh*. The *Gemara* (Pesachim 118a) says that a person who speaks or even believes *lashon hara* deserves to be thrown to the dogs. That no dog barked was an indication that the original sin has been corrected, if only temporarily.

5770

Rabbi Yitzchak Salid – *Shabbat Parah* always immediately precedes *Shabbat HaChodesh*, which is an aberration in the conventional logic of Jewish calendar. The laws of the *Parah Adumah* deal with removing *tumah*, which is generally contracted through laziness and being less than careful about what one touches. *HaChodesh* heralds the pre-*Pesach* period where we are uber-observant and careful in ridding our dwellings of *chametz* and in preparing the *matzah* in the prescribed manner. The homiletic message is an exhortation to overcome our spiritual laziness and <u>immediately</u> transition to scrupulous adherence to the *Torah* to prepare for our imminent redemption.

5772

Rabbi Yossi Jankovits – Why, except in a leap year, when there is a second *Adar*, is Parashat Tzav always read on *Shabbat HaGadol*, immediately prior to *Pesach*? Perhaps this is because Tzav outlines the *Korban Todah*, which is brought based on having survived one of four dangerous occurrences: (1) getting out of prison; (2) crossing a sea; (3) crossing a desert and (4) recovering from an illness. These bases for the *Todah* can be recalled by the acronym "חיים," where the "cheit" stands for "cholim," or "sick persons," the "yud" stands for "yisurim," or "captives," the second "yud" stands for "yam," or "sea," and the "mem" stands for "midbar," or "desert." These elements were all at work in the Exodus story, for which *Bnei Yisrael* must show gratitude on *Pesach*. We, in chronological order, (1) got out of jail (*Mitzrayim*); (2) crossed the *Yam Suf*; (3) crossed the *midbar*; and (4) at *Har Sinai*, experienced a *refuah* for all maladies and illnesses the Jews had at that time. (Midrash Rabbah Vayikra 18:4)

Rabbi Abraham Stone – There are *Abra'ah Leshonot Geulah* – Hashem, in Parashat Va'eira tells *Moshe* "v'hotzeiti," "and I will take you out"; "v'hitzalti, "and I will rescue you"; "v'ga'alti," "and I will redeem you"; and "v'lakachti," "and I will take you [for Me]." (Shemot 6:6, 7) It is well known that we drink four cups of wine to commemorate these four statements, but why wine specifically, and not four *matzot*, for example? The first three expressions represent leaving the exile of Egypt and are, in fact, tied to the *matzot*, but the fourth term refers to a free People gathered at *Matan Torah*, an event of a higher transcendent level that requires wine to celebrate, not "poor man's bread." Since the fourth item of remembrances must therefore be wine, we use wine to commemorate all four terms.

5773

On *Chol HaMoed Pesach* and *Sukkot*, why do we say "moadim l'simcha; chagim u'zemanim l'sasson," which translates to "holidays <u>towards</u> happiness, festivals and times <u>towards</u> happiness?" Wouldn't it be more appropriate to say "moadei simcha, chagim u'zemanim sasson," "happy holidays, festivals and times of happiness?" We add "towards" to show that the holidays are meant to create happiness that continues on after the holidays conclude.

Rabbi Ephraim Sprecher – There is a fifth expression beyond the *Arba'ah Leshonot Geulah* of "v'heiveiti," in the *pasuk* "and <u>I shall bring</u> you to a Land that I swore to Avraham, Yitzchak and Yaacov." (Shemot 6:8) The Rambam (Hilchot Chametz Umatza 8:10) accordingly mentions using a fifth cup at the *Pesach Seder* for the fifth expression, but views it as optional. Rabbi Menachem Mendel Kasher strongly advocates drinking from a fifth cup by passing the *Kos shel Eliyahu*. He believes that since we are privileged to live in a time when the fifth expression has been realized, it is only appropriate to express our gratitude and thanks, and to fail to do so would show a lack of *hakarat hatov*.

Rabbi Yitzchak Isaac Chaver – While *Yaacov* was surely intent on being buried in *Eretz Yisrael*, due, in part, to the *kinim* that would one day plague the soil of *Mitzrayim* (Rashi on Bereshit 47:29), his concern was not that his remains would be desecrated by the lice. Rather, he was concerned that the *Kedushah* of his remains would keep the lice from the soil around his *kever*, thereby minimizing the breadth and the glory of the *makah*. As with the other *makot* and the *Torah's* insistence on ensuring that there would be no opening for the *Mitzrim* to question the Power of *Hashem*, there could be no questions raised with regard to the *Makat Kinim*.

SHAVUOT

5757

There is a distinction in the *Bereshit* narrative describing the six days of Creation. For the first five days, the day is not preceded with a letter "heh," but the sixth day does include the "heh," and reads "יוֹם הַשִּׁשִּׁי," "the sixth day." (Bereshit 1:31) *Chazal* tell us that the first five days represent the five books of Moses, and the emphasis of the *Talmud* (Avodah Zareh 3a) on the sixth day represents the sixth day of *Sivan*, which is *Shavuot*, "z'man mattan Torahteinu," "the Season of the Giving of our Torah."

5758

Iturei Torah - On *Shavuot* we read *Megillat Rut*, the story of Judaism's most famous convert. The *gematria* of "רות," "Rut" is 606. Birkei Yosef states that this is an allusion to the fact that *Rut*, as a gentile, was already bound by and observant of the *Sheva Mitzvot Bnei Noach*. In accepting the entirety of the *Torah*, Rut added 606 *mitzvot* for a total of 613.

The *Gemara* (Pesachim 68b) relates that every year on *Shavuot Rav Yosef* would prepare a lavish feast, saying "אי לא האי יומא דקא גרים כמה יוסף איכא בשוקא," "But for this Day [of Matan Torah], how many 'Yosefs' would be in the marketplace?" *Rav Yosef's* rhetorical question could be understood as "if I did not have the *Torah*, I'd be just another 'Joe' in the marketplace," but perhaps more accurately, it could mean "if not for adopting an unwavering *Torah* standard of conduct, I would be a different 'Yosef' in the marketplace!" Living a life guided by the timeless principles of the *Torah* ensures that one's conduct is consistent, whether he is at home, at shul or at his place of business.

5759

In *Megillat Rut*, Boaz instructs *Rut* "v'cho vicho tidbaki im na'arotai," "so stay here and cleave to my maidens." (Rut 2:8) Yet later in the narrative we learn "וַתֹּאמֶר רוּת הַמּוֹאֲבִיָּה גַּם | כִּי אָמַר אֵלַי עִם הַנְּעָרִים אֲשֶׁר לִי תִּדְבָּקִין עַד אִם כִּלּוּ אֵת כָּל הַקָּצִיר אֲשֶׁר לִי," "And Rut the Moaviah said, '[Boaz] also said to me; You shall stay with my young men until they finish my entire harvest.'"

(Rut 2:21) Significantly, where *Rut* improperly makes reference to Boaz's "young men" rather than his "maidens," the *Megillah* refers to her as "Rut the Moabite." The question arises: why the improper recounting of the words of *Boaz*? The Midrash Rabbah (Rut 2:9, 5:11) indicates that *Rut* was still a Moabite at the time of this recounting and had not, as is commonly understood, converted to Judaism prior to her arrival in *Eretz Yisrael*. The Midrash Rabbah (*perush* of Maharzu) states, however, that *Rut* was either still imbued with the immorality of the *Moav* nation or that she made a linguistic mistake common to one who is becoming accustomed to a gender laden language such as Hebrew. This later explanation seems to be more defensible given her demonstrated modesty in the narrative (Shabbat 113b) and *Naomi's* tactful correction in the next verse. (Rut 2:22) It is indisputable that for the *geir* a constant effort is necessary to integrate properly and completely into the *Tzibbur*. This effort transcends learning Jewish jargon, but permeates all areas of the life of the observant Jew. This recalls a *vort* from Rabbi Yissocher Frand, who draws a lesson from the counting of the *Omer*. When a Jew fulfills the *mitzvah* of counting the days between *Pesach* and *Shavuot* he mentions both the number of days counted and the number of weeks counted to date. Rabbi Frand suggests that there is a lesson in this counting for both the "*frum* from birth" Jews as well as newly observant *baalei teshuvah* and *geirim*. The always observant Jews have no trouble connecting to the Jewish Community. Having grown up in *Yiddishkeit*, it is natural to participate in the communal aspects of Judaism. What is often missing is a meaningful one-on-one relationship with *Hashem*. Such Jews would do well to focus on the individuality expressed in the count of days. For the newly observant, their journey to Judaism often begins with the realization of *Hashem* and the initiation of a relationship with Him. However as with *Rut*, the newly observant often struggle to integrate into and contribute to the larger Jewish community. Such Jews would do well to focus on the collective as expressed in the counting of weeks.

Megillat Rut informs us that Rut arrived in Eretz Yisrael at the beginning of the barley harvest (Rut 1:22) and that "וַתִּדְבַּק בְּנַעֲרוֹת בֹּעַז לְלַקֵּט עַד כְּלוֹת

"קְצִיר הַשְּׂעֹרִים וּקְצִיר הַחִטִּים וַתֵּשֶׁב אֶת חֲמוֹתָהּ," "she stayed with Boaz's maidens to glean until the completion of the barley harvest and the wheat harvest, and she dwelt with her mother-in-law." (Rut 2:23) This is a ninety-day period, from which the Midrash Rabbah (Rut 5:11) says was established a ninety-day waiting period after which a new convert may marry a Jew. Chazal determined that a convert is not free of the remnant of impurity until three months following conversion. Mishneh Torah (Gerushin 10:21) indicates this *halachah* applies to female converts to remove any questions concerning pregnancy before conversion.

Shavuot celebrates the giving and, importantly, acceptance of the *Torah*, which prompts *Chazal* to compare all of *Bnei Yisrael* to *geirim*, who likewise accept the "yoke" of *Torah*. The Rambam (Hilchot Issurei Biah 13:4) indicates that the convert to Judaism does three things in the conversion process that mirror the actions of the Jews in the Exodus: (1) *milah* – which *Bnei Yisrael* did before leaving *Mitzrayim* (Shemot 12:48); (2) *mikvah* – which *Bnei Yisrael* did before *Matan Torah* (Ibn Ezra on Shemot 19:10); and (3) *korban* – which *Bnei Yisrael* brought after *Matan Torah* (Shemot 24:5).

Maharal - The *Gemara* (Shabbat 88a) describes how in His Giving of the *Torah*, *Hashem* held *Har Sinai* over the heads of the Jewish People, indicating that their decision not to accept the *Torah* would result in their destruction, in essence forcing their acceptance. *Talmud Yerushalmi* (Rosh Hashanah 1:3) tells us that *Hashem*, so to speak, has bound Himself to the *mitzvot* of the *Torah*. Therefore, as in a case of a rape, where the *Torah* dictates that the man "may never send her away all the days of her life," (Devarim 22:29), since *HaKadosh Baruch Hu* coerced *Bnei Yisrael* concerning *Torah* acceptance, He can never send us away, no matter how bad our infractions.

5760

The Rema (Shulchan Aruch O.C. 494:3) cites many reasons offered for the strong *minhag* of eating dairy on *Shavuot*, the holiday of Receiving the

Torah. The *gematria* of "חלב," milk, is forty, and *Moshe* was on *Har Sinai* receiving the *Torah* for forty days. (Shemot 24:18) Also, Mishnah Berurah (494:12) teaches that when the Jews received the *Torah* they became *chayav* in the laws of *kashrut*, including *shechitah*. Lacking the proper *kaylim* to prepare meat meals immediately after the Divine Revelation, they ate a milk meal which was more easily prepared. Rabbi Yitzchak Lipietz adds that *Batyah bat Paroh* drew baby *Moshe* out of the water on the sixth of *Sivan* (Iturei Torah states he was born on seven *Adar* and was hidden for three months (Shemot 2:2)), which coincides with *Shavuot*, and because *Moshe* would only nurse from a Jewish woman (who happened to be his mother *Yocheved* [Shemot 2:9]), we recall this occurrence by eating a milk meal on that date. (Sefer Matamim)

Rabbi Yossi Jankovits – The central issue of the later part of *Megillat Rut* is whether *Boaz* could marry *Rut*, a Moabite woman. There is a *halachah* from the *Torah* prohibiting marriage between Jews and Moabites based on the lack of hospitality displayed by *Bnei Moav* when the Jews were traveling in the desert. (Devarim 23:4, 5) *Boaz* had to convene a *minyan* for a *Beit Din* to learn out the lesser known *halachah* (Yevamot 77b) that Moabite women were allowed to marry into *Bnei Yisrael* as they were in their homes during the incident in question, and it was only the Moabite men who refused to resupply the Jews. Even later in Jewish history, however, the question remained as to the status of female Moabite converts and, accordingly, *Rut* and her progeny. As a result of this *halachic* question, *Rut's* grandson *Yishai* assumed his sons born to his Jewish wife had a questionable pedigree based on *Rut* having Moabite blood. The *Midrash* (Sefer HaToda'ah; Yalkut HaMachiri) explains that *Yishai* wanted to ensure that his seed would fulfill its mission to bring the *Mashiach* to the Jewish people, so he therefore arranged to have relations with a gentile slave woman by which to father a child. While the boy initially would be 100% gentile, *Yishai* could thereafter convert the child to Judaism, making him unquestionably Jewish in having no halachic connection to *Moav*. *Yishai's* wife thought to foil his plan and instead conspired to stand in for the slave woman and have relations with

Yishai herself. *Yishai* was unaware of the substitution and was therefore doubly surprised when the slave woman did not conceive but his wife did. When his wife bore *David*, *Yishai*, who, to his mind, had not been with her, assumed he was a *mamzer*. When *Shmuel HaNavi* came to *Yishai's* home to ordain one of his children King of Israel, it never occurred to *Yishai* that *David* could qualify. When *Shmuel* failed to choose *Yishai's* older sons and was insistent that there must be another son who was the rightful heir to the throne, *Yishai* understood that his wife was righteous, and that *Rut's* status as a legitimate convert was unquestionable. (I Shmuel 16:5-13)

5761

Rabbi Eli Mansour - The story of *Rut* is read on *Shavuot* to underscore that the Jews received the entire *Torah* on *Har Sinai*, including the *Oral Law*. The entire controversy of *David's* lineage is resolved in the *Gemara* (Yevamot 77a) as a *Halachah l'Moshe m'Sinai*. Without the *Torah Shebaal Peh*, we would think *David* is forbidden to be the progenitor of the *Mashiach* as the product of a marriage to a Moabite woman in seeming contradiction to the *Torah Shebichtav*. (Devarim 23:4, 5)

5762

Rabbi Yochanan Zweig – The *Gemara* (Yevamot 62b) tells us that 12,000 pairs of students of *Rabbi Akiva* died during the period of *Sefirat HaOmer* because they were disrespectful to each other as *talmidei chachamim*. The period of *Sefirat HaOmer* is about acceptance of the entire *Torah*, including the *Oral Law*. This is evidenced in the *machloket* as to when to start counting the *Omer*. The *pasuk* in Parashat Emor states "וּסְפַרְתֶּם לָכֶם מִמָּחֳרַת הַשַּׁבָּת מִיּוֹם הֲבִיאֲכֶם אֶת עֹמֶר הַתְּנוּפָה שֶׁבַע שַׁבָּתוֹת תְּמִימֹת תִּהְיֶינָה," "And you shall count for yourselves, from the morrow of the 'shabbat' from the day you bring the omer as a wave offering seven weeks; they shall be complete." (Vayikra 23:15). Only by virtue of the *Oral Torah* (Menachot 66a) do we know that "shabbat" in this context means the day after the first day of *Pesach* and not the first

Shabbat that follows *Pesach*. A *talmud chacham* is arguably greater than a *Sefer Torah*, as he knows both the *Oral and Written Torah*. Disrespecting such a person is the opposite of the goal of the *Sefirat HaOmer* period, which is to move toward acceptance of the entire *Torah* on *Shavuot*.

5763

Rabbi Moshe Weinberger — The second day of *Sivan*, when *Bnei Yisrael* had encamped at *Har Sinai* in preparation for *Matan Torah*, is referred to as "Yom HaMiyuchas," "the Day of Distinguished Lineage." On that day (Rashi on Shemot 19:3) *Hashem* instructed *Moshe* "וְאַתֶּם תִּהְיוּ לִי מַמְלֶכֶת כֹּהֲנִים וְגוֹי קָדוֹשׁ אֵלֶּה הַדְּבָרִים אֲשֶׁר תְּדַבֵּר אֶל בְּנֵי יִשְׂרָאֵל," "'And You shall be to Me a Kingdom of Princes and a Holy Nation.' These are the words that you shall speak to the Children of Israel." (Shemot 19:6) With regard to *yichus*, the *Gemara* (Shabbat 67a) tells us that *Rabbi Shimon Bar Yochai* is of the opinion "kol Yisrael Bnei Melachim heim," "every Jew is the Son of the King," with the independent power to rule over his *yetzer hara*. Additionally, Rabbi Tzadok HaKohen explains the Jewish People emanate from a barren woman, *Sarah*, and therefore our entire existence is miraculous. This is the powerful combination: free will and the ability to overcome seemingly insurmountable obstacles. This is the *yichus* of the Jewish People, something worth contemplating as *Shavuot* approaches.

Rabbi Chaim Flom — The Midrash Rabbah (Rut 2:14) states that *Megillat Rut* was incorporated into *Tanach* to teach Jews the great reward for doing *chesed*. *Rut* was rewarded for her treatment of *Naomi* with being the progenitor of the House of *David* and, ultimately, the *Mashiach*!

Rabbi Yossi Jankovits - The Chasam Sofer states that the connection between *Shavuot* and the Parashat Nasso, which is read proximate to the holiday, is that *Galiyat*, the enemy of *David*, is the product of *Orpah* (*Rut's* sister/sister in law), who is mentioned in *Megillat Rut*, which is read on *Shavuot*, and *Shimshon*, whose birth is mentioned in the *Haftarah* for Nasso. (Shoftim 13:2-25)

5764

Rabbi Moshe Weinberger - *Rut* is the *tikkun* for *Lot*. *Lot* decided to separate himself from *Avraham Avinu* to be elevated as a *macher* in *S'dom* (Bereshit 13:12). Conversely, *Rut* decided to leave her exalted life as a Moabite princess to become a poor Jew who picked up *leket* and *shichah* in the field of *Boaz*. (Ruth 2:3) Lot's progeny were *Bnei Moav*, who were barred from entering in the Congregation of *Hashem*, in part, because of their refusal to give Jews bread in the desert (Devarim 23:5), which displayed a lack of *hakarat hatov*, insofar as their ancestor *Lot* had been saved by the Jew's ancestor *Avraham*. (Bereshit 14:16) *Rut*, herself a Moabite, went with her Jewish mother-in-law *Naomi* to "Beit Lechem," "House of Bread." (Rut 1:19)

5765

Yossi Hahn - The contention that *Megillat Rut* is read on *Shavuot* to demonstrate the binding nature and importance not only of the *Written Law* but also of the Oral Tradition is bolstered by the entire episode of the supposed "levirate marriage" between *Boaz* and *Rut*. In a very telling verse, the *Megillah* states "וְזֹאת לְפָנִים בְּיִשְׂרָאֵל עַל-הַגְּאֻלָּה וְעַל-הַתְּמוּרָה, לְקַיֵּם כָּל-דָּבָר, שָׁלַף אִישׁ נַעֲלוֹ, וְנָתַן לְרֵעֵהוּ; וְזֹאת הַתְּעוּדָה, בְּיִשְׂרָאֵל," "Now this was the custom in former times in Yisrael concerning redemption and exchange, to confirm anything, one would remove his shoe and give it to his fellow, and this was the ratification in Yisrael." (Rut 4:7) This verse is the basis upon which *Boaz*, before marrying *Rut*, had to offer the field of *Elimelech* (*Rut's* deceased father-in-law) and *Rut's* hand in marriage to a certain relative, referred to in the *Megillah* as *Ploni Almoni*. *Boaz* was constrained to do so insofar as *Ploni Almoni* was closer than *Boaz* in blood relation to *Elimelech*, which entitled him a first refusal right to acquire the land and *Rut* as a required package deal. This is clearly not a case of *yibum* as described in the *Torah* (Devarim 25:5-10), which applies only in the case where one brother dies childless and his surviving brother marries his widow. What the *Megillah* is describing is a *minhag* of the Jewish Nation in place at the time, which was accepted and observed by the Jews of that generation. The binding effect of *minhagim* is a central theme of *Shavuot*, when we recognize that the body of binding Jewish legal tradition goes far beyond the *Chamishah Chumshay Torah*.

Rabbi Yossi Jankovits – The *Gemara* (Shabbat 86b) records the dispute amongst *Chazal* as to whether the Giving of the *Torah* actually occurred on the sixth or seventh day of *Sivan*. The *Torah* mandates that the holiday of *Shavuot*, which celebrates *Matan Torah*, be observed on the sixth of *Sivan* (Vayikra 23:15-21), yet in deference to the other opinion we call Shavuot "zman Matan Torahteinu," "the period [rather than day] of the Giving of Our Torah."

5766

Rabbi Eli Mansour - In Parashat Vayeira, *Avraham* is visited by three "men" following his *brit milah*. (Bereshit 18:2) There, Rashi states that these were three angels, each sent by Hashem for a specific mission: *Rafael* to heal *Avraham*, *Michael* to inform *Sarah* of the impending birth of *Yitzchak*, and *Gavriel* to destroy *S'dom*. (Rashi on Bereshit 18:1, 2) Rabbi Mansour asks why *Gavriel* needed to accompany the others to *Avraham* and *Sarah*, who did not reside anywhere near *S'dom*. He also questions the *pasuk* describing an exchange between the angels and *Avraham*. "וַיֹּאמְרוּ אֵלָיו אַיֵּה שָׂרָה אִשְׁתֶּךָ וַיֹּאמֶר הִנֵּה בָאֹהֶל," "And they said to him, 'Where is Sarah your wife?' And he said, 'Behold in the tent.'" (Bereshit 18:9) The angels in this case were asking *Avraham*, the model of all humanity, as to what is the proper *derech* of women with regards to guests. *Avraham*, who experienced *Ruach HaKodesh*, understood the question had cosmic importance to the future of mankind. (Rashi on Bereshit 18:9; Yevamot 77a) In the days of *David HaMelech*, there was a question as to *David's* lineage, based on the fact that his great-grandmother was *Rut*, a convert from the nation of *Moav*. The *Written Torah* expressly prohibits a Moabite from marrying a born Jew, in part because *Moav* did not provide *Bnei Yisrael* with bread and water during their travels in the desert. (Devarim 23:4, 5) The *Oral Law* received by *Moshe* on *Har Sinai* and passed to the Jews through subsequent generations indicates that this prohibition applies to the men of *Moav* but not to the women (Yevamot 77a), because it is the way for women to remain in their tents, it being immodest to go out to attend to visitors and travelers. The angels therefore ask *Avraham* about Sarah to confirm how a woman should act. It was necessary for *Gavriel* to obtain this understanding, in order to confirm that it was necessary to save *Lot*, the progenitor of *Moav*, before destroying *S'dom*. *Lot* was destined to give rise to *Moav* and would, through *Rut* (who, as a woman was not barred from conversion and marriage to *Boaz*), father the royal Davidic dynasty and ultimately the Holy *Mashiach*. MRF Note – Perhaps it was not for the *malach* to <u>learn</u> the *halachah* of the women of *Moav* but to <u>teach</u> the *halachah* through his visit. Would it make sense for the *malach* to learn whether or not to save *Lot* when the *Torah*, which existed before the Creation of the world, indicates that *Amon* and *Moav* may not join *Am Yisrael*? Presumably these nations were destined to descend from *Lot*, so had he been destroyed there would have been an inconsistency between *Torah*, the blueprint for reality, and reality itself. But perhaps the story of *Sarah* in the tent gave support in the enduring rabbinical controversy to those who argued that the law of the acceptance of *Moav* women was a *Halachah l'Moshe m'Sinai*, the position that ultimately prevailed.

5768

According to the *Yerushalmi* (Chagigah 2:3), *David HaMelech* was born and died on *Shavuot*. It is interesting to note the many instances of righteous women taking decisive action in bringing about the creation of the Davidic Dynasty and sowing the seeds of *Mashiach*. For instance, *Lot's* daughters took affirmative steps to repopulate the world, believing it had been destroyed. (Bereshit 19:30-38) As described in *Megillat Rut*, *Rut*, *David's* great-grandmother, clearly took action in following *Naomi*, converting to Judaism and marrying *Boaz*. *Tamar* orchestrated her relationship with *Yehudah* (Bereshit 38:1-24), and his son *Peretz* was an ancestor of *Boaz* and therefore *David*. (Rut 4:18-22) The *Midrash* relates that even *David's* mother *Nitzevet* (Bava Batra 91a) herself took the place of her husband *Yishai's* maidservant in order to take an active role in the Messianic vision. (Sefer HaToda'ah; Yalkut HaMachiri) Rabbi Aharon Lichtenstein states that the *Midrash* (Shemot Rabbah 28:1) on *Tehillim* (68:19) teaches that the *Torah* was and must always be taken by force. In each of these cases, women of valor took decisive and often difficult steps to ensure the ultimate salvation of all mankind through the *Torah*.

5769

Rabbi Yitzchak Salid – The admonitions of the *Torah* appear in Parashat Bechukotai and Parashat Ki Tavo, in each case preceding by two weeks (rather than one week) *Shavuot* and *Rosh Hashanah*, respectively. In both cases the warnings are required to properly prepare us for the essential aspects of these days, but we are not able to hear about the horrors of noncompliance with *Hashem's* Will on the *Shabbat* immediately preceding these *Yom Tovim*. One important message is that *Shavuot* has the awesome nature of *Rosh Hashanah* and should not be treated lightly.

Rabbi Eliyahu Kitov – The *pasuk* in *Megillat Rut* states "וַתָּשָׁב נָעֳמִי וְרוּת הַמּוֹאֲבִיָּה כַלָּתָהּ עִמָּהּ הַשָּׁבָה מִשְּׂדֵי מוֹאָב וְהֵמָּה בָּאוּ בֵּית לֶחֶם בִּתְחִלַּת קְצִיר שְׂעֹרִים," "So Naomi returned, and Ruth the Moaviah, her daughter-in-law, with her <u>returned</u> from the fields of Moav-and they came to Beit Lechem at the beginning of the barley harvest." (Rut 1:22) Clearly *Naomi* was returning to *Eretz Yisrael*, the Land of her origin, but how so for *Rut*, a Moabite princess who presumably had never been there? The *Torah* describes *Rut* as "returning" to Israel because although she was a convert by *halachah*, she was, in fact, returning to the Source of her essence. *Rut* was one of the souls "made" by *Avraham Avinu* and *Sarah* (Bereshit 12:5), returning to the Land after 700 years. Rut possessed the spark of Avraham that was the *chesed tikkun* for Elimelech, who ran from *chesed* and removed his family from their native Land during the famine. (Rut 1:1, 2) The idea that a *geir* "returns" to Judaism is presented by the Ohr HaChaim (Devarim 21:11), who teaches that there are sparks of *Kedushah* spread throughout the world. When *Adam HaRishon* ate from the *Eitz HaDa'at*, the result was a scattering throughout the world the "sparks of light" that were once singly sourced with him. Gentiles who possess one of these sparks of *Kedushah* seek out Jews, who form the group that is closest to G-d and contains the largest concentration of *Kedushah* in the world. These gentiles seek to cleave to the Jews so as to return to the source of their being, and to match the *Kedushah* spark within them to the larger source. This is the sole reason for the *galut*. According to the Baal Shem Tov, Jews must inject themselves into the world at large in order to "redeem" these Holy sparks.

5770

Rabbi Yossi Jankovits - The Midrash Rabbah (Rut 6:1) draws a clear comparison between the episode of *Yaacov* receiving the favored *berachah* from *Yitzchak* (Bereshit 27:18-29) and *Rut* coming to the threshing floor where *Boaz* lay. (Rut 3:7-14) In both cases a righteous matriarch (*Rivkah* and *Naomi*, respectively) understood the enormity of the situation and orchestrated the optimal outcome. Additionally, in each case the righteous progenitor of the Jewish People (*Yaacov* and *Rut*, respectively) dutifully followed the counsel for the matriarch to bring about the desired outcome. Finally, in each case the patriarchal participant (*Yitzchak* and *Boaz*, respectively) was gripped with shuddering when the enormity of the moment in Jewish history was revealed. Specifically, when the substitution of *Yaacov* for *Eisav* became known to *Yitzchak*, the *Torah* tells us "vayecherad Yitzchak," "and Yitzchak trembled," (Bereshit 27:33), which Rashi describes both as fear and astonishment. The *Megillah* informs us that when *Boaz* discovered *Rut* near him, "vayecherad haish," "and the man trembled," (Rut 3:8) perhaps also through an appreciation of the seriousness and importance of the moment.

5771

Rabbi Yechezkel Shraga Halberstam – The *pasuk* says "וְקִדַּשְׁתֶּם אֵת שְׁנַת הַחֲמִשִּׁים שָׁנָה וּקְרָאתֶם דְּרוֹר בָּאָרֶץ לְכָל יֹשְׁבֶיהָ יוֹבֵל הִוא תִּהְיֶה לָכֶם וְשַׁבְתֶּם אִישׁ אֶל אֲחֻזָּתוֹ וְאִישׁ אֶל מִשְׁפַּחְתּוֹ תָּשֻׁבוּ," "And you shall sanctify the year of the fiftieth year and proclaim liberty in the Land for all its inhabitants; it shall be a Jubilee Year for you, you shall return each man to his ancestral heritage and you shall return each man to his family." (Vayikra 25:10) Why is the *Yovel* referred to as the "year of the fiftieth year?" *Yovel* can be compared to *Shavuot*. During *Sefirat HaOmer* we are supposed to advance in steps of Holiness towards a proper receiving of the *Torah*, yet if one fails to prepare he can actually make up for the entire *Omer* period on the fiftieth day (i.e. *Shavuot*). Similarly, the repetition of the word "year" in the *pasuk* indicates that in one year a person can attain everything he should have learned in the preceding forty-nine years (and seven *Shemittah* years). The Rambam (Hilchot Teshuvah 2:1) actually says that *teshuvah* at the end of one's life is accepted. But, one may ask, does that opportunity exist for all of *Bnei Yisrael*? The remainder of the *pasuk* provides the answer: it is an ancestral heritage for all Jews.

5772

Reb Roy S. Neuberger – In *Megillat Rut*, *Boaz* comforts *Rut* by saying "וְעַתָּה כִּי אָמְנָם, כִּי אִם גֹּאֵל אָנֹכִי; וְגַם יֵשׁ גֹּאֵל, קָרוֹב מִמֶּנִּי לִינִי הַלַּיְלָה, וְהָיָה בַבֹּקֶר אִם־יִגְאָלֵךְ טוֹב יִגְאָל, וְאִם־לֹא יַחְפֹּץ לְגָאֳלֵךְ וּגְאַלְתִּיךְ אָנֹכִי, חַי־ הי; שִׁכְבִי, עַד־הַבֹּקֶר," "And now it is true that I am a Redeemer; however there is a redeemer nearer than I . . . Remain this night, and it shall be in the morning, that if he will redeem you, well; let him redeem you; but if he is not willing to redeem you, then I [swear] I will redeem you. Lie down until the morning." (Rut 3:12) The Ben Ish Chai emphasizes that these are not merely the words of *Boaz* to *Rut* but of *Hashem* to *Am Yisrael*. He assures us that the night of exile will end. The "closer redeemer" is our own *mitzvot* and *maasim tovim*. They can bring *Mashiach* before the appointed time. "But do not fear," says *Hashem*, "for if not, I will redeem you."

5773

Rabbi Shmuel Rabinowitz — In describing the scene at *Har Sinai* prior to *Matan Torah*, the *Torah* relates that "v'yachan sham Yisrael," "and Israel encamped there." (Shemot 19:2) There Rashi, in reconciling the singular form of the verb "encamped," famously describes the Jews "כאיש אחד בלב אחד," "as if a single man, with one heart." The unity that *Am Yisrael* achieved at *Har Sinai* was unprecedented and hugely valuable, independent of the Giving of the *Torah*. This is the basis of the declaration in the "Dayeinu" song of the *Haggadah* that if *Hashem* had brought us to *Har Sinai* but had not given us the *Torah* it would still have been sufficient to thank Him. Ever since that seminal moment, *Am Yisrael* has been striving, with limited success, to replicate that *achdut*, but it inspires us nonetheless to know we are capable as such unity as a Nation.

5777

Rabbi Yossi Jankovits - There is a *machloket* set forth in the *Gemara* (Pesachim 68b) as to the proper way for a Jew to use his time on *Yom Tov*. Rabbi Eliezer holds that one may either devote the day to eating and drinking for his personal benefit or, alternatively, may spend the entire day engaged in *Torah* learning. Rabbi Yehoshua famously says "'חלקהו חציו לה וחציו לכם," "Divide [the day] as half for Hashem and half for [the Jews]," which is the final *halachah* on the matter. (Shulchan Aruch O.C. 529:1) The *Gemara* goes on to explain that all agree with Rabbi Yehoshua with respect to the *Yom Tov* of *Shavuot*, and states "מ"ט יום שניתנה בו תורה," "what is the reason? [Shavuot] is the date on which the Torah was Given." (Pesachim 68b) The choice of *Shavuot* as the only *Yom Tov* that Rabbi Eliezer would concede requires *gashmiut* in the form of eating and drinking is surprising. One may have expected either the holiday of *Sukkot* or *Pesach* as most conducive to physicality. Indeed, why is the holiday celebrating the Giving of the *Torah* less conducive to learning *Torah* rather than more? The *Gemara* (Shabbat 88b) relates the incident by which *Moshe* ascended to Heaven to take the *Torah* for *Bnei Yisrael*. The *malachim* objected that the treasured *Torah* should be given to mere human beings. *Hashem* directed *Moshe* to answer the angels, and *Moshe* proceeded to list all the *mitzvot* of the *Torah* that are directed to human beings exclusively, including, for example, engaging in business transactions, honoring one's parents and overcoming the *yetzer hara*. (Shabbat 89a) This idea, that the *Torah* is meant for humans rather than angels, proved to be the winning argument that made *Matan Torah* on *Shavuot* possible. Accordingly, it is specifically on *Shavuot* that we are required to celebrate with food and drink in order to underscore the merits of *Moshe's* argument.

TISHA B'AV

5758

Rabbi Chaim Shmuelevitz - In Parashat Devarim, which is read on the *Shabbat* immediately preceding *Tisha B'Av, Moshe* rebukes *Bnei Yisrael* by listing all the places that they sinned, but only alluding to their actual sins. (Rashi on Devarim 1:1) This approach contains a *mussar* message that is a central principle of interpersonal communications. We should rebuke only as necessary and never derive enjoyment from it. This is an important lesson to internalize in the days preceding *Tisha B'Av* when the Second Temple was destroyed because of baseless hatred amongst Jews.

5759

The *Talmud* explains that the *Three Weeks* of mourning between *Shiva Asar b'Tammuz* and *Tisha B'Av* correspond to the three hours that *Adam HaRishon* did not wait before partaking of the Tree of Knowledge of Good and Evil. (Sanhedrin 38b) The Lubavitcher Rebbe (Lekutei Sichot: chelek 24-page 133) states that had *Adam* waited, it would have been *Shabbat* and he would have had permission to eat it.

5760

Rabbi Yisroel Ciner – The *Talmud* (Yoma 69b) tells us that *Yirmiyahu HaNavi*, upon seeing the nations rejoicing at the destruction of the *Beit HaMikdash* left out "norah," "awesome," in describing *Hashem*. Daniel, upon seeing the nations enslave *Bnei Yisrael*, left out "gibor," "powerful." When the *Men of the Great Assembly* codified the *Shemoneh Esrei* they included reference to *Hashem* as "HaGadol (the Big), HaGibor (the Strong) v'HaNorah (the Awesome)." The *Men of the Great Assembly* lived at the end of the Babylonian Exile, following the *Purim* miracle. Their inclusion of these references to *Hashem* conceded the point well understood by *Yaacov*: that our ups and downs are awesome displays of *Hashem's* Power and Greatness.

5761

Tisha B'Av is closely tied to the story in the *Gemara* (Gittin 56a) about "Kamtza and Bar Kamtza." *Chazal* tell us that because of the incident of *Kamtza* and *Bar Kamtza* the Temple was destroyed. A party invite intended for *Kamtza* was inadvertently received by *Bar Kamtza*, who came nonetheless, was thrown out of the party by the host, and then set about to destroy the host and the attending rabbis who did nothing to protest his humiliating expulsion. We can understand why *Bar Kamtza* is blamed; after all he was involved in the *machloket* that spiraled out of control. But why would *Kamtza* be blamed? He never received the original party invitation! The problem with *Kamtza* is that he was socially connected to people like the party's host that were capable of excluding and publicly embarrassing other Jews. Such social associations helped fertilize the soil in which *sinat chinam* could grow, thereby making *Kamtza* guilty through that association.

5763

Rabbi Aviezer Heller – Contrary to normative *halachah*, one could marshal an argument for allowing learning on *Tisha B'Av*. The *Gemara* (Taanit 30a) tells us that children would be off from school on *Tisha B'Av* (implying they were otherwise in school year-round), which could be viewed as a pleasurable thing, as Ramban (in the name of Tosafot on Shabbat 116a) tells us that *Bnei Yisrael* departed from *Har Sinai* as would children leaving school (i.e. eager and with delight). We might think that so too an adult would receive no pleasure from studying a difficult *sugya*, and therefore it would be *mutar* on *Tisha B'Av* to learn in such a way. To the contrary, the Aruch HaShulchan (Orach Chayim 554:3) explains that the soul of a Jew connects to *Torah* at all times and receives *hanaah*, even when his mind may be put off from the subject or difficulty. It is that soulful pleasure that is prohibited to us on *Tisha B'Av*.

5764

Rabbi Yossi Jankovits - There is a well-known idea that *Hashem* continually remakes the world to bring *geulah* and unlimited *Kedushah* to *Bnei Yisrael*. He also created the *satan* to be vigilant in looking for means to reduce *Bnei Yisrael* and deprive us of opportunities to elevate ourselves and achieve our noble destiny. Therefore, *Hashem* orchestrates good for the Jewish People through unsuspected, unlikely, and even immoral channels. This is evident in Parashat Masai, when *Hashem* sets forth the boundaries of *Eretz Yisrael*. (Bamidbar 34:1-13) Like any land survey, it begins with a "point of beginning," where it also ends. Here, the "POB" is "Yam HaMelach," the "Salt Sea," what we know as the Dead Sea. One could question why something as exalted as *Eretz Yisrael* should be surveyed with such a prominent dismal primary reference, for the Dead Sea recalls the cities of *S'dom* and *Amorah*, and the incident of *Lot* and his daughters. (Bereshit 19:30-38) Because the *satan* seeks to foil *Mashiach's* emergence, the *Torah* hides the settling of *Eretz Yisrael*, a glorifying precondition for the ultimate redemption, in the unseemly reference to the Dead Sea, and connects the Land to *Lot*, who gave rise to *Moav*, from whom *Rut* came, who is the progenitor of *David HaMelech*, from whom our Redeemer will ultimately emerge. Similarly, *Hashem* saw fit to bring the seeds of redemption through *Tamar* and *Yehudah* and *David* and *Batsheva*. In fact, there is a *mesorah* recorded in the *Talmud* Yerushalmi (Berachot 2:4) that *Mashiach Tzidkeinu* will be born on *Tisha B'Av*, thereby bringing us towards the final redemption through a sad, and therefore unexpected, origin.

5765

Rabbi Edward Davis – Parashat Devarim is always read on "Shabbat Chazon," the *Shabbat* that falls during the *Nine Days* and which immediately precedes *Tisha B'Av*. The *Midrash* (Eichah: intro) tells us that, following the decree that all males from ages twenty to sixty would die in the desert (and thus never enter the Promised Land), a macabre annual event took place every *Tisha B'Av*. All men subject to the decree would dig a grave and lay down within it overnight on *Tisha B'Av*. In the morning, those who were destined to die that day would be buried, and those who woke up would return to their homes. Significantly, the tribe of *Levy*, which was not subject to the decree (not having a representative who participated in the sin of the *meraglim*), nonetheless undertook the same ritual annually. Why would the men of *Levy* go through the trouble of digging a grave and lying within if they were not designated to die on that day? The answer is that *Levy* wanted to physically empathize with their distressed brothers. By participating in the annual event, they demonstrated the importance of *achdut* among the Jewish People. Regardless as to how one feels about the Disengagement/Expulsion of Jews from *Gush Katif*, it is necessary for every Jew to empathize with their plight and to say *kinot* on their behalf.

5771

Rabbi Neal Turk - Rav Soloveitchik held that the *Three Weeks* period was an inverse of the progression of *aveilut* upon the death of a loved one (G-d forbid). The *Three Weeks* of National mourning correspond to the twelve months of personal mourning, the *Nine Days* correspond to the thirty day *shaloshim* period, and *Tisha B'Av* corresponds to the intensive seven day *shivah* period. Based on this understanding, the *dinim* of each stage may be reexamined. Because one is permitted to shave during the year of mourning (following the *shaloshim*), students of the Rav shave during the *Three Weeks*. Yet because a party of any kind is prohibited for the year of *aveilut*, these students would not have a party, even without music, during the same *Three Weeks* period. The points are (1) one needs to be consistent in following a particular *halachic* model and, more importantly, (2) during this time of year we need to internalize the concept that we are involved in a communal, yet very real, *aveilut*, based on having lost our Holy Temples.

5772

Rabbi Abraham Stone – The *Navi Yishaiyah* declared "שִׁמְעוּ שָׁמַיִם וְהַאֲזִינִי אֶרֶץ כִּי הי דִבֵּר בָּנִים גִדַּלְתִּי וְרוֹמַמְתִּי וְהֵם פָּשְׁעוּ בִי," "Hear, O Heavens, and give ear, O earth, for Hashem has spoken: 'Children I have raised and exalted, yet they have rebelled against Me.'" (Yishaiyah 1:2) Daat Zakainim notes that the word "haazinu," "give ear," indicates closer proximity than "shimu," "hear," which suggests that *Yishaiyah* was closer to the earth than the Heavens. This is in distinction to the *pasuk* from Parashat Haazinu when *Moshe* declares the reverse: "הַאֲזִינוּ הַשָּׁמַיִם וַאֲדַבֵּרָה וְתִשְׁמַע הָאָרֶץ אִמְרֵי פִי," "Give ear, O Heavens, and I will speak; and may the earth hear the words of my mouth." (Devarim 32:1) For the Heavens, *Moshe* uses the word "haazinu," and for the earth, "tishma," indicating that he was closer spiritually to the Heavens than the earth. Daat Zakainim comments that this presents a problem. While we might expect that *Moshe* was closer to Heaven and *Yishaiyah* was closer to earth, if an exalted prophet such as *Yishaiyah* was "bound to earth" in distinction to *Moshe*, what should the average Jew feel about his spiritual level and potential? The Shelah HaKadosh answers by noting the time of year each *Navi* is read. The prophesy of *Yishaiyah* is read on *Tisha B'Av*, when we are farthest from *Hashem*. Haazinu, which is read during *Aseret Yemei Teshuvah*, informs us that at that time of year *Hashem* is nearest to us, all of us, not merely *Moshe Rabbeinu*, which is *chizuk* to redouble our efforts in *teshuvah* and *tzedakah*.

5773

The Slonimer Rebbe - We can ask a strong question with respect to the destruction of *Bayit Sheni*, which the *Mishnah* (Taanit 4:6) tells us occurred on *Tisha B'Av*. The *Gemara* (Yoma 9b) tells us that the cause of the destruction was *sinat chinam*, yet nowhere in the *Torah* is "baseless hatred" described as a sin worthy of such a severe punishment. How can it be that *Hashem* destroyed the Holy Temple and exiled *Am Yisrael* on this basis? The answer lies in the fact that the *churban* is not a punishment for *sinat chinam*, but a consequence of it! The supernatural structure of the

Holy Temple requires *achdut* among the Jews as a foundational prerequisite. Struggles between Jews break the connection between Heaven and earth, without which those stones cannot remain standing. This provides a powerful insight into how we must proceed as a Nation after *Tisha B'Av* if we genuinely wish to rebuild the Temple.

CHART CONVERTING HEBREW YEAR TO COMMON ERA YEAR

Hebrew Year	Fall to Summer of
5757	1996-1997
5758	1997-1998
5759	1998-1999
5760	1999-2000
5761	2000-2001
5762	2001-2002
5763	2002-2003
5764	2003-2004
5765	2004-2005
5766	2005-2006
5767	2006-2007
5768	2007-2008
5769	2008-2009
5770	2009-2010
5771	2010-2011
5772	2011-2012
5773	2012-2013
5774	2013-2014
5775	2014-2015
5776	2015-2016
5777	2016-2017

GLOSSARY OF TERMS, PLACES AND PERSONS

Achashveirosh (King): King in the *Purim* story, as mentioned in *Megillat Esther*

achdut: unity

Adam (HaRishon): man (the first)

Adar: twelfth (sixth) month in Hebrew calendar, during which *Purim* is celebrated

Adar Sheni: "Second Adar"; additional *Adar* inserted into Jewish leap year (7 times in 19 years) to ensure *Nissan* falls out in spring as commanded by the *Torah*

ad meiah v'esrim: "until 120 [years]"

Afikoman: dessert *matzah* at end of the *Pesach Seder*; substitute for *Korban Pesach*

Aggadah / Aggadita: non-legal texts or stories set forth within the *Oral Law*

Aharon (HaKohain): Aaron (the Priest), brother of *Moshe*; first *Kohain Gadol*

Akeidah (Akeidat Yitzchak): the Binding (of *Yitzchak*); *Hashem* tells *Avraham* to offer his son as a sacrifice

Al HaNisim: additional prayer added to *Shemoneh Esrei* and *Birkat HaMazon* in thanks to *Hashem* on *Chanukah* and *Purim*

aliyah / aliyot: "going up"; refers both to going up to read from the *Torah* and emigration to Israel

amah / amot: cubit(s); measurement

Amalek: a nation that descended from Amalek, son of *Eisav*; attacked *Bnei Yisrael* in the desert and we are commanded to destroy them and their memory. *Haman* was a descendant of Amalek

am haaretz: "people of the land"; an uneducated person

Am HaNivchar: "Chosen Nation"; the Jewish People

Amidah / Amidot: the main section of daily prayer also known as *Shemoneh Esrei*

Am Kadosh: "Holy Nation"; the Jews

Amon: a nation that battled against *Bnei Yisrael* in the desert; descended from *Lot*

Amora: scholar of the period from about 200 to 500 CE, who "said" or "told over" the teachings of the Oral Torah

Amram: husband of *Yocheved*; father of *Moshe*, *Aharon* and *Miriam*

Am Yisrael: the Nation of Israel

Anaini HaKavod : Clouds of Glory; protected Jews in the desert

aravot: willow branches; one of the *Arba'ah Minim* of *Sukkot*

Arba'ah Minim: "Four Species"; taken as a *mitzvah* on *Sukkot*: lulav, etrog, hadassim and aravot

Arba'ah Leshonot Geulah: four expressions of redemption in the *Torah*

Aretz: "Land"; Land of Israel

Aron (Kodesh): (Holy) Ark, in the *Beit HaMikdash* and also located in the *shul*, which houses the *Sifrei Torah*

Aseret Yemei Teshuvah: "Ten Days of Repentance"; ten days between and including *Rosh Hashanah* and *Yom Kippur*

Ashkenaz / Ashkenazim: *nusach* pertaining to the Jews of middle and eastern Europe; Jews who follow Ashkenaz *nusach*

assur: forbidden

atzeret: "assembly"; in the *Gemara*, *Shavuot*

Av: fifth (eleventh) month of the Hebrew calendar, during which *Tisha B'Av* occurs; or father

aveirah / aveirot: transgression(s) of a *Torah* law

Avinu Malkeinu: "Our Father, Our King"; prayer recited *Aseret Yemei Teshuvah* and fast days

avodah: service

avodah zareh: idol worship

Avodat Hashem : worship and service of *Hashem*

Avot: "Patriarchs"; *Avraham, Yitzchak* and *Yaacov*

Avraham (Avinu): Abraham (our Father); husband of *Sarah*; father of *Yitzchak* and *Yishmael*

Aza: Gaza

Azaryah: with *Chananyah* and *Misha'el*, defied *Nevuchadnezair*

Azazael: the entity to whom the "scapegoat" is offered on *Yom Kippur*

baal/baalat/baalei teshuvah: "master(s) of return"; one(s) who adopt(s) a *Torah* lifestyle later in life

Bar Kamtza: character from the *Gemara* story of the cause of the destruction of *Bayit Sheni*

Bar Mitzvah: "Son of the Commandment"; a male who has attained the age of thirteen and is therefore *chayav* in the *mitzvot*

bashert: spouse predestined by Heaven

bas Melech: "daughter of the King"

Bat Mitzvah: "Daughter of the Commandment"; a female who has attained the age of twelve and is therefore *chayav* in the *mitzvot* of women

Batyah (bat Paroh): daughter of *Paroh*, found *Moshe* in the river and adopted him

Bavel: Babylon

Bayit Sheni: "second House"; the second *Beit HaMikdash*

Be'er Miriam: "Well of *Miriam*"; miraculously provided water in the *midbar*

Beit HaMikdash / Batei Mikdash: the First or Second Temple(s)

ben sorer u'moreh: rebellious son

berachah / berachot: blessing(s)

Bereshit (Sefer Bereshit): "in the beginning"; Book of Genesis; the first Book (and first *parashah*) of *Chamishah Chumshay Torah*

Betuel: father of *Lavan* and *Rivkah*

Bigtan: eunuch in *Purim* story that conspired with *Teresh* against *Achashveirosh*

Bilhah: wife of *Yaacov*; maidservant of *Rachel*; mother of *Dan and Naftali*

Binyamin: Benjamin; youngest son of *Yaacov* and *Rachel*; one of the *Twelve Tribes*

Birkat HaMazon: "Blessing of Food"; grace after meals

bitachon: trust (in *Hashem*)

Bnei Moav: children of Moab

Bnei Yisrael: Children of Israel

Boaz: married *Rut*

bris: *brit milah*

brit milah: "covenant of circumcision"; ritual circumcision on the eighth day of life; also known as a *bris*

Caleiv (ben Yefuneh): Caleb (son of Yefuneh); one of the twelve spies sent to *Eretz Yisrael* from the desert; husband of *Miriam*

Chabad (Lubavitch): *chassidic* sect involved in worldwide *kiruv*

Chacham(im): Sage(s); also wise son in *Haggadah*

Chag / Chagim: festival(s)

challah: braided bread loaf in honor of *Shabbat* or *Yom Tov*

chametz: products made from five grains that are prohibited on *Pesach*

Chamishah Chumshay Torah: "Five Sections of the Torah"; the Pentateuch; five books of the *Torah* organized in order of weekly *Parshiot*

Chananyah: with *Azaryah* and *Misha'el*, defied *Nevuchadnezair*

Chanukah: eight day holiday celebrating the rededication of the *Bayit Sheni*; Festival of Lights

chanukiah: eight branched *menorah* lit on *Chanukah*

Chashmonaim: dynasty of Kohanim during and after the Chanukah story

chassid(im) / chassidut / chassidishe / chassidic: "pious one(s)"; hassidic; movement founded in eighteenth century Eastern Europe by the Baal Shem Tov

chas v'shalom: "G-d forbid"

Chavah: first woman; married *Adam*

chaveirah tovah: good friend

chayav: guilty of transgressing; obligated

Chazal: acronym of "Chachameinu Zichronam Levrachah," "Our Sages of blessed memory"

chazan: leader of prayer service

cheit haeigel (hazahav): sin of the (golden) calf

chenek: strangulation; a form of capital punishment

chesed: loving kindness towards others

chiddush / chiddushim: novel *Torah* insight(s)

chizuk: encouragement

chok / chukat / chukim: *Torah* law(s) or *mitzvah (mitzvot)* for which no explanation is provided

Chol HaMoed: intermediate days of *Pesach* and *Sukkot* where some work is permitted

Chumash: *Chamishah Chumshay Torah*

chumrah / chumrot: stringency(ies) beyond *halachah*

chuppah: marriage canopy

Chur: Hur; son of *Miriam* and *Caleiv*

churban: "destruction"; the destruction of the *Beit HaMikdash*

chutz l'Aretz: "outside the Land"; outside of *Eretz Yisrael*

chutzpah: audacity, brazenness

Daf Yomi: "page of the day"; refers to the practice of studying one page of *Gemara* a day, and finishing the entire *Talmud* in a seven and a half year cycle

dam: blood; first Egyptian plague

Dan: son of *Yaacov* and *Bilhah*; one of the *Twelve Tribes*

davash: honey

daven (davening): to pray (praying); *tefillah*

David (HaMelech): "King David"; second king of Israel, credited with writing most of Sefer Tehillim, progenitor of the *Mashiach*

Dayeinu: "it would have sufficed"; song of praise to *Hashem* in *Haggadah*

derech: manner; way; path

din (dinim): law(s); judgment(s)

Dinah: daughter of *Yaacov* and *Leah*

dreidel: four-sided spinning top played on *Chanukah*

d'var Torah / divrei Torah: "word(s) of Torah"; thought-provoking *Torah* idea; *vort*

Eisav: Esau, twin brother of *Yaacov*; son of *Yitzchak*

Eitz HaDa'at: "Tree of Knowledge"; produced fruit consumed by *Adam* and *Chavah*

Eliezer: servant to *Avraham*

Elimelech: in *Megillat Rut*, husband of *Naomi*, father-in-law of *Rut*

Eliyahu HaNavi: Elijah the Prophet

Elul: sixth (twelfth) month of the Hebrew calendar

emet: true

emunah: faith (in *Hashem*)

Ephraim: son of *Yosef*; became like one of the *Twelve Tribes*

Eretz Yisrael: Land of Israel

erev: "evening of"; the day proceeding *Shabbat or Yom Tov*

Erev Rav: non-Jews who accompanied the Jews out of *Mitzrayim*

Erev Shabbat: "eve of *Shabbat*"; Friday before sundown

Esther: heroine of *Megillat Esther* and the *Purim* story

etrog: citron; one of the *Arba'ah Minim* of *Sukkot*

eved Hashem: "servant of G-d"

frum: devout; fully observant of *halachah*

Galiyat: Goliath; killed by *David*; son of *Orpah*

galut: exile, the Diaspora

Gan Ayden: Garden of Eden

gashmiut: "materiality"; in contrast to spirituality

Gavriel: Gabriel; a *malach*

gebrochtz: *matzah* soaked in water, use for cooking which some *Ashkenazim* and *chassidim* avoid on *Pesach*

Gemara: *Talmud Bavli*

geir / geirim: convert(s)

gematria: tradition of interpreting meanings and significance by totaling the numerical equivalents of Hebrew letters

geulah: redemption or deliverance

Givon: an ancient Canaanite city north if *Yerushalayim*

goy / goyah / goyim: gentile(s); female gentile; non-Jew(s)

grogger: spinning noisemaker used on *Purim* to drown out *Haman's* name

guf: body

Gush Katif: Israeli settlement in *Aza*, destroyed in August 2005 with displacement of 8,600 Jewish residents

hadassim : myrtle; one of the *Arba'ah Minim* of *Sukkot*

Hadran Alach: "We Will Return"; prayer recited at a *siyum*

Haftarah / Haftarot: selected section from *Naviim*, recited following the weekly *Torah* reading on *Shabbat* and *Yom Tov*

Hagar: maidservant of *Sarah*; when *Sarah* could not conceive she gave *Hagar* to *Avraham*; mother of *Yishmael*

Haggadah: "narration"; the book used to conduct the *Pesach Seder*

hakarat hatov: "recognizing the goodness"; gratitude

HaKadosh Baruch Hu: *Hashem*

halachah / halachot / halachic: (pertaining to) *Torah* Law(s)

Halachah l'Moshe m'Sinai: "Law from Moshe at Sinai"; law whose source is not written but was transmitted orally from *Hashem* to *Moshe*

Hallel: "praise"; *tefillot* recited on *Rosh Chodesh* and *Chagim*

HaMakom: "the Place"; *Hashem*

Haman: the villain of *Megillat Esther* and the *Purim* story

hamantaschen: cookie served on *Purim*

hanaah: pleasure

Har Moriah: site of *Akeidat Yitzchak*

Har Sinai: "Mount Sinai"; where the *Torah* was given

Hashem: "the Name"; G-d

Hashgachah Pratit: concept that every event is determined by Divine Will

hatzalah: rescue

Havdalah: prayer to mark the conclusion of *Shabbat* and *Yom Tov*

Hillel (HaZakein): "(the Elder)"; Sage of the *Talmud* with *Shammai* last of *Zugot*

Hoshana Rabbah: seventh day of *Sukkot* when extra *aravot* are taken and waved

inyan / inyanim: topic(s), center(s) of interest

issur: prohibition

Iyar: second (eighth) month of Hebrew calendar

Kabbalah / Kabbalistic: (pertaining to) Jewish mysticism

Kamtza: character from the *Gemara* story of the cause of the destruction of *Bayit Sheni*

kashrut: state of being kosher; *halachot* of kosher

kavanah: concentration; intention

Kedushah: Holiness; essential prayer in repetition of *Shemoneh Esrei*

kehillah: congregation

keli / kaylim: utensil(s)

keter: crown

Ketuvim: "writings"; the third division of the *Tanach*

kever / kevarot: grave(s)

Kiddush: prayer recited at the beginning of a festive meal on *Shabbat* and *Chag*

Kiddush Hashem: sanctification of the name of *Hashem*; martyrdom

kikar: unit of weight, approximately sixty five pounds

kinim: lice; third Egyptian plague

kinot: "lamentations"; read on *Tisha B'Av*

kiruv: Jewish educational outreach to unaffiliated Jews

Kislev: ninth (third) month of Hebrew calendar

Klal Yisrael: the Jewish community as a whole

Kodesh HaKadoshim: "Holy of Holies"; inner sanctuary of the *Mishkan* and *Beit HaMikdash*

Kohain / Kohanim: Priest(s); descendants of *Aharon*

Kohain Gadol: High Priest

Kohelet: Book of Ecclesiastes, part of *Tanach*

kollel: "gathering"; an institute for full-time advanced *Torah* study

Kol Nidre: "all the vows"; opening prayer for *Yom Kippur*

Korach: cousin of *Moshe* and *Aharon* who led a revolt against them

korban / korbanot: sacrifice(s) offered in the *Mishkan* and *Beit HaMikdash*

Korban Pesach: Passover sacrifice during Temple times

Korban Todah: Thanksgiving sacrifice

Kos shel Eliyahu: "Cup of Elijah"; a fifth cup poured at the *Seder*

Kriyat Yam Suf: Splitting of the Sea of Reeds

Lag B'Omer: thirty-third day of the *Omer*; festive day between *Pesach* and *Shavuot*

lashon: tongue; language

lashon hara: word (or non-verbal communication) that is either derogatory or potentially harmful to another

Lavan: brother of *Rivkah*; father of *Rachel* and *Leah*

Leah: daughter of *Lavan*; sister of *Rachel*; wife of *Yaacov*; mother of *Reuven, Shimon, Levy, Yehudah, Yissachar, Zevulun* and daughter *Dinah*

leket: fallen gleanings during the harvest that must be left for the poor

levayah: funeral

Levy: son of *Yaacov* and *Leah*; one of the *Twelve Tribes*

Lot: nephew of *Avraham*

Luchot: Tablets; the Stones upon which were transcribed the Ten Commandments

lulav: palm branch; one of the *Arba'ah Minim* of *Sukkot*

Maariv: evening prayer service

maasim tovim: good deeds

Maccabi(m): "Maccabee(s)"; the Jewish army of rebel(s) in the *Chanukah* story

macher: person of influence

machloket: disagreement, debate

makah / makot: plague(s)

malach / malachim: angel(s), messenger(s)

Malchiot: "Kingship" portion of *Mussaf* for *Rosh Hashanah*

mamzer: child resulting from relations between a Jewish man and a Jewish woman who are forbidden to marry one another

Maoz Tzur: poem sung on *Chanukah*

maror: bitter herbs eaten at the *Pesach Seder*

mashal: example, allegory

Mashiach (Tzidkeinu): "Messiah (the Righteous One)"; bringer of the ultimate redemption

Mashiach ben David: "Messiah, son of (King David)"; from Tribe of *Yehudah*

Mashiach ben Yosef: "Messiah, son of (Tribe of) Joseph"

matanot l'evyonim: "gifts to the poor"; cash distributed on *Purim*

Matan Torah: "the Giving of the *Torah*" at *Har Sinai*; celebrated on *Shavuot*
Matityahu ben Yochanan HaKohain: leader of *Maccabim* in *Chanukah* story
matzah / matzot: unleavened bread(s) eaten on *Pesach*
mayim: water
mechillah: forgiveness
megillah: scroll
Megillat Esther: "Scroll of Esther"; read on *Purim*
Megillat Rut: "Scroll of Ruth"; read on *Shavuot*
melech: king
Menashe: son of *Yosef*; brother of *Ephraim*; became like one of the *Twelve Tribes*
Menorah: Candelabra used in the *Mishkan* and *Beit HaMikdash*
meraglim: spies
mesorah: tradition
midbar: desert
middah / middot: attribute(s) of character
middah keneged middah: "measure for measure"; the principle of "what goes around comes around," as directed by *Hashem*
Michael: an angel
Midrash / Midrashim: non-legal commentary and interpretative teaching(s)
miKadaish Shem Shamayim: "to sanctify the Name of Heaven"
mikvah: ritual bath
milah: *brit milah*
Minchah: afternoon prayer service; or flour offering
minhag / minhagim: binding custom(s), as opposed to *halachah*
Miriam: sister of *Aharon and Moshe*; wife of *Caleiv*; mother of *Chur*
Misha'el: with *Azaryah* and *Chananyah*, defied *Nevuchadnezair*
Mishlei: Book of Proverbs, part of *Tanach*
Mishkan: Tabernacle; portable sanctuary used in the *midbar*; replaced by the *Beit HaMikdash*
mishloach manot: "sending of portions"; gifts of food sent on *Purim*
Mishnah: first written compilation of *Oral Law*, divided into six *sedarim*

Mitzrayim / Mitzri /Mitzrim: Egypt; Egyptian(s)
mitzvah / mitzvot: commandment(s) of the *Torah*
Mizbeach: Altar in the *Mishkan* or *Beit HaMikdash*
Moav / Moavim: Moab; (land of) nation descended from *Lot*; Moabites
modim: "we thankfully acknowledge"; a blessing in the *Shemoneh Esrei*
Mon : Manna; miracle food that fell daily in the *midbar*
Mordechai: hero of *Megillat Esther* and the *Purim* story
Moshe (Rabbeinu): Moses (our Teacher)
muktzeh: items forbidden by the Rabbis to be moved on *Shabbat*
Mussaf: additional prayer service recited on *Shabbat, Yom Tov, Chol HaMoed*, and *Rosh Chodesh*
mussar: morality, ethics, methods for personal improvement in character
nachat / nachas: spiritual satisfaction and pleasure
Naftali: son of *Yaacov* and *Bilhah*; one of the *Twelve Tribes*
Naomi: mother-in-law of *Rut*
Navi / Naviim: Prophet(s); second division of the *Tanach*
Nevuchadnezair: Babylonian king, destroyed the first *Beit HaMikdash* and exiled the Jews
nefesh: in *Kabbalah*, the lowest level of the human soul
Neilah: "closing"; the closing service of *Yom Kippur*
ner / neirot: candle(s)
neshamah / neshamot: soul(s)
Nine Days: first nine days of the month of *Av*, during which there is a National period of mourning
Nissan: first (ninth) month of the Hebrew calendar
Nishmat Kol Chai: "the soul of every living thing"; prayer recited on *Shabbat* and *Yom Tov*
Nitzevet: mother of *David*; wife of *Yishai*
nun: fourteenth letter of the Hebrew alphabet
nusach: particular style of prayer or religious custom
Olam HaEmet: "the World of Truth"

Olam HaZeh: this world

Omer: formal counting of forty-nine days between *Pesach* and *Shavuot,* named for the Temple grain offering

oneg: delight, spiritual pleasure

Oral Law: laws, statutes and legal interpretations that were not recorded in *Chamishah Chumshay Torah* but given to *Moshe* at *Har Sinai*; includes *Talmud, Mishnah* and *Gemara*

orlah: fruit of a tree prohibited for the first three years after planting; a covering

Orpah: sister and sister-in-law of *Rut*; mother of *Galiyat*

Parah Adumah: "Red Heifer," used in Temple times to purify after contact with a corpse

parashah / parashat / parshiot: *Torah* portion(s)

Paroh: "Pharaoh"; Egyptian king

pasuk / pasukim: verse(s)

patur: exempt

Peretz: son of *Yehudah* and *Tamar*; ancestor of *Boaz* and *David*

perush: commentary to clarify original text

Pesach: Passover, festival commemorating Exodus from Egypt

pizmon: extra-liturgical poem contained in *Selichot*

Ploni Almoni: "so-in-so"; relative of *Elimelech* in *Megillat Rut*

poskin / posek: Render a *halachic* decision; one who *poskins*

Potiphar / Potiphera: one of *Paroh*'s officials who acquired *Yosef* as a slave

Purim: "lots"; holiday of 14 *Adar* celebrating the victory over *Haman*

Rabbah: Rabbah bar Nachmani; third and fourth century C.E. *Amora* in *Bavel*

Rabbi Akiva: Akiva Ben Yosef, *Tanna* in latter part of first century

Rabbi Eliezer: second generation *Tanna*; teacher of *Rabbi Akiva*

Rabbi Meir: *Tanna,* student of *Rabbi Akiva*

Rabbi Shimon bar Yochai: Rashbi; second century *Tanna*

Rabbi Yehoshua ben Chaninah: first century *Tanna*

Rabbi Yehoshua ben Levy: third century *Talmudic* Scholar

Glossary of Terms, Places and Persons — 153

Rabbi Yehudah: Yehuda bar Ilai, second century *Tanna*

Rabbi Yehudah HaNasi: second-century rabbi and chief redactor and editor of the Mishnah

Rabbi Zeira: third generation *Amora* in *Bavel* and *Eretz Yisrael*

Rachel: daughter of *Lavan*; sister of *Leah*; wife of *Yaacov*; mother of *Yosef* and *Binyamin*

Rafael: an angel

Ramses: territory in Egypt

rashei teivot: Hebrew abbreviation based on first letter of each word of a phrase

Ratzon Hashem: the Will of G-d

Rav: scholar, teacher

Rava: Rabbi Abba ben Joseph bar Chama; fourth generation *Amora* in *Bavel*

Rav Nachman: third generation C.E. Amora in Bavel

Rav Yosef: third generation C.E. Amora in Bavel

Rebbe: *Torah* teacher; head of *chassidut* sect

rebbetzin: wife of a rabbi

refuah: healing

Reuven: son of *Yaacov* and *Leah*; one of the *Twelve Tribes*

Rivkah: daughter of *Betuel*; sister of *Lavan*; wife of *Yitzchak;* mother of *Yaacov* and *Eisav*

Rosh Chodesh: "head of the month"; one or two semi-festive day(s) when new moon appears marking the beginning of each month

Rosh Hashanah: "head of the Year"; Jewish New Year; first day of *Tishrei*

ruach: spirit; in *Kabbalah*, a part of the human soul

Ruach HaKodesh: "Divine Spirit"; prophecy

ruchniut: spirituality

Rut: Ruth, *Moavi* princess who converted to Judaism; married *Boaz*; *Megillat Rut* is part of *Tanach*

safek: doubt

Sarah (Imeinu): Sarah (Our Mother); wife of *Avraham*; mother of *Yitzchak*

satan: accuser, Heavenly prosecutor

s'chach: natural material used for the roof of a *sukkah*

S'dom (and Amorah): Biblical cities Sodom (and Gomorrah)

sedarim: orders (of the *Mishnah*)

Seder: "order"; the festive meal on *Pesach*

sefer / sifrei / sefarim: book(s)

Sefer Torah: *Torah* Scroll

Sefirah (Sefirat HaOmer): "counting"; counting of *Omer* for forty-nine days between *Pesach* and *Shavuot*

selichot: "forgiveness"; penitential prayers said in the week before *Rosh Hashanah* and during *Yamim Noraim*

se'or: leaven; prohibited on *Pesach*

seudah: meal

seudat mitzvah: a celebratory meal connected to performance of a *mitzvah* or a *siyum*

Shabbat / Shabbatot: Sabbath(s); Day(s) of Rest

Shabbat HaChodesh: "Sabbath of the Month"; *Shabbat* preceding month of *Nissan*

Shabbat HaGadol: "Great Sabbath"; *Shabbat* preceding *Pesach*

Shabbat Parah: "Sabbath of the [Red] Heifer"; *Shabbat* before *Shabbat HaChodesh*, *Torah* portion describing *Parah Adumah* is read

Shabbos: Sabbath; *Shabbat*

Shacharit: morning prayer service

shalom: peace; hello; or goodbye

shalom bayit: "peace in the home"; a superlative Jewish virtue

shaloshim: thirty day mourning period following burial

Shalosh Regalim: three annual pilgrimage festivals: *Pesach*, *Shavuot* and *Succot*

shalvah: serenity

Shamayim: Heaven

Shammai: first century Sage of *Mishnah*; with Hillel last of *Zugot*

Shavuot: "Feast of Weeks"; the holiday commemorating the giving of the *Torah*

Shechinah: Divine Presence

shechitah / shecht / shechted: ritual animal slaughter

shehakol: blessing for certain standard foods

Shehecheyanu: prayer of gratitude for special occasions

shekel: coin in the Temple era; Israeli coin

Shema (Yisrael): "Hear (Israel)"; daily prayer declaration of faith recited at *Shacharit* and *Maariv*

Shemini Atzeret: "Eighth Day of Assembly"; holiday immediately following *Sukkot*

Shemittah: "sabbatical year"; seventh year of agricultural cycle when the land lies fallow

Shemoneh Esrei: "Eighteen" benedictions; also known as *Amidah*, main section of daily prayer service

Sheva Mitzvot Bnei Noach: "Seven Laws of the Children of Noah"; universal obligations binding all people including non-Jews

Sheva Berachot: "Seven Blessings" recited at a Jewish wedding and at each of the seven festive meals that follow

Shevet / Shevatim: Tribe(s) descended from the twelve son(s) of *Yaacov*

shibud: enslavement

shichah: "forgotten bundles" from the harvest that must be left for the poor

shidduch: match or arranged marriage

Shimon: son of *Yaacov* and *Leah*; one of the *Twelve Tribes*

Shimshon: Samson; one of the Judges

shir / shirah: song

Shiva Asar b'Tammuz: seventeenth day of the month of *Tammuz*, a fast day; beginning of the *Three Weeks*

shivah: week-long mourning period for first-degree relatives: father, mother, son, daughter, brother, sister, and spouse

Shlomo (HaMelech): (King) Solomon

shloshim: thirty day mourning period marked with eulogies

Shmuel HaNavi: Samuel the Prophet; the last of the Judges

shmurah matzah: "guarded matzah" made from grain that is supervised from the harvesting through the baking process

Shoah: the Holocaust

shochet: ritual slaughterer

shofar: ram's horn blown of *Rosh Hashanah* and *Yom Kippur*

Shofrot: "Horns" portion of *Mussaf* for *Rosh Hashanah*

shoresh: root, origin

shul: synagogue

Shulchan: ceremonial Table in the *Mishkan* and *Beit HaMikdash*

Shushan (HaBirah): Shushan (the Capital); venue of the *Purim* story

Shushan Purim: holiday of 15 *Adar* celebrating the victory over *Haman* in *Shushan*; today celebrated only in *Yerushalayim*

Siddur: Jewish prayer book

simchah / simchas: joyous occasion(s); or happiness

Simchat Beit HaShoeivah: "Celebration of the Water Drawing"; water pouring ceremony on *Sukkot* in *Beit HaMikdash*

Simchat Torah: "Rejoicing with the *Torah*"; holiday that immediately follows *Sukkot*; second day of *Shemini Atzeret* in the Diaspora

Simchat Yom Tov: "Happiness on the Holiday"; the *mitzvah* to be joyful on every holiday

Sinai: mountain in the desert where the *Torah* was given

sinat chinam: baseless hatred

Sisra: commander of the Canaanite army

Sivan: third (ninth) month of the Hebrew calendar; month of *Shavuot*

siyum: completion of any unit of *Torah, Mishnah* or *Talmud*; often accompanied by a festive meal

skilah: stoning; form of capital punishment

sofit: "ending"; special form of certain Hebrew letters appearing at the end of a word

sugya: unit of organization of the *Gemara*

sukkah/ sukkot: temporary structure(s) for dwelling in the *midbar* and during *Sukkot*

Sukkot: "Feast of Tabernacles"; holiday in month of *Tishrei* celebrated with *sukkot* and *Arba'ah Minim*; also territory in *midbar*

Talmud (Bavli): most widely used repository of *Oral Law*, composed in Babylonia; *Gemara*

talmud chacham / talmidei chachamim: *Torah* scholar(s)

Tamar: daughter-in-law and wife of *Yehudah*

Tammuz: fourth (tenth) month in Hebrew calendar

Tanach: *rashei teivot* of *Torah, Naviim* [and] *Ketuvim*; the three parts of the *Torah*

Tanna / Tannaim: scholar(s) from the *Mishnah* period

tefillah / tefillot: prayer(s); *davening*

Tefillin: "phylacteries"; ritual objects worn on the forehead and arm by men during *Shacharit*

Tehillah / Tehillim: Psalm(s); part of *Tanach*

Teresh: eunuch in *Purim* story that conspired with *Bigtan* against *Achashveirosh*

teruah: sound blast of a *shofar*

teshuvah: repentance

Three Weeks: twenty-one day National mourning period between the fast days of *17 Tammuz* and *Tisha B'Av*

tikkun: improvement, correction

Tisha B'Av: "Ninth of Av"; fast day commemorating the destruction of the first and second *Batei Mikdash*

Tishrei: first (seventh) month of the Hebrew calendar

Torah: "teaching"; broadly refers to the written and oral history and laws given at *Sinai* and thereafter, including *Tanach*; narrowly, *Chamishah Chumshay Torah*

Torah Shebaal Peh: "The *Oral Law*"; also given to *Moshe* at *Har Sinai* with *Chamishah Chumshay Torah*

Torah Shebichtav: "The *Written Law*"; *Chamishah Chumshay Torah*

Tosefet Shabbat: "adding to Shabbat"; the *mitzvah* to extend *Shabbat* beyond twenty-four hours both on Friday afternoon and Saturday night

tumah: impurity

Twelve Tribes: *Shevatim*

tzaddik (gamor) / tzaddikim: (completely) righteous one(s)

Tzibbur: Community, Congregation

tzorchei Tzibbur: needs of the Community

U'Netana Tokef: "let us speak of the awesomeness"; prayer on *Rosh Hashanah* and *Yom Kippur* that precedes *Kedushah* in *Mussaf*

Ushpizin: "guests"; seven patriarchal figures welcomed into the *sukkah*

Vashti: first wife of *Achashveirosh*; predecessor to *Esther* in *Purim* story

vav: sixth letter of the Hebrew alphabet

vort: "word"; thought-provoking *Torah* idea

Written Law: *Torah* laws set forth in *Chamishah Chumshay Torah*

Yaacov (Avinu): Jacob (our Father); son of *Yitzchak*; husband of *Leah* and *Rachel*; father of the *Shevatim* and daughter *Dinah*

Yael: woman who killed *Sisra*

Yehoshua (bin Nun): Joshua (son of Nun); student of Moshe; second leader of *Bnei Yisrael* who conquered *Eretz Yisrael*

yahrzeit: anniversary of a death

Yamim Noraim: "Days of Awe"; High Holy Days of *Rosh Hashanah* and *Yom Kippur*

Yam Suf: "Sea of Reeds"; where the Jews were saved and the Egyptians drowned

Yarden: Jordan (River)

Yehoshua: Joshua, *Moshe's* successor; or Book of Joshua, part of *Tanach*,

Yehudah: Judah; son of *Yaacov* and *Leah*; one of the *Twelve Tribes*

yemach shemo / yemach shemam: may his (their) name be obliterated

Yerushalayim: Jerusalem, Israel!

Yerushalmi (Talmud): the version of *Talmud* compiled in *Eretz Yisrael* in the fourth century

yeshivah: Torah academy

yeshuah / yeshuot: salvation(s)

yetzer hara: evil inclination

yibum: levirate marriage whereby brother marries childless dead brother's widow

yichus: distinguished family status or pedigree

Yiddishkeit: Jewishness; Judaism

Yirmiyahu: Jeremiah the *Navi*; part of *Tanach*

Yishaiyah (Yishaiyahu): Isaiah the *Navi*; part of *Tanach*

Yishmael: Ishmael; son of *Avraham* and *Hagar*; brother of *Yitzchak*

Yisrael: *Yaacov Avinu*; also sometimes referring to *Bnei Yisrael*

Yissachar: Issacher; son of *Yaacov* and *Leah*; one of *Twelve Tribes*

Yitzchak (Avinu): Isaac (our Father); son of *Avraham*; husband of *Rivkah*; father of *Yaacov* and *Eisav*

Yocheved: wife of *Amram*; mother of *Moshe*

Yom HaDin: "Day of Judgment"; final judgment after death or *Rosh Hashanah*

Yom Kippur: "Day of Atonement"; fast day Festival on tenth of *Tishrei*

Yom Tov / Yom Tovim: "Good Day(s)"; Jewish holiday(s)

Yonah: Jonah

Yosef (HaTzaddik): Joseph (the Righteous); son of *Yaacov* and *Rachel*; father of *Ephraim* and *Menashe*; one of the *Twelve Tribes*

yud: tenth letter of the Hebrew alphabet

Zecharyah: sixth century *Navi* in *Bavel*, part of *Tanach*

zechut: merit

Zevulun: Zebulun; son of *Yaacov* and *Leah*; one of *Twelve Tribes*

Zichronot: "Remembrance" portion of *Mussaf* for *Rosh Hashanah*

Z'man Cherotainu: "the Time of our Freedom"; *Pesach*

Z'man Matan Torateinu: "the Time of the Giving of our Torah"; *Shavuot*

Z'man Simchateinu: "the Time of our Happiness"; *Sukkot* and *Shemini Atzeret/ Simchat Torah*

Zugot: "Pairs"; paired religious scholars during the time of *Bayit Sheni*

SOURCES & INFLUENCES

Abramsky	Rabbi Yechezkel	(1886-1976); Belarus; *Chazon Yechezkel*
Admor of Gur		Rabbi Yaakov Aryeh Alter; Yerushalayim, Israel; seventh Rebbe of Ger
Aruch HaShulchan		Rabbi Yechiel Michel Epstein; (1829-1908); Lithuania
Aruch LaNer		Rabbi Yaacov Ettlinger; (1798-1871); Germany
Assouli	Rabbi Yitzchak	Yerushalayim, Israel
Baal HaTurim		Rabbi Jacob Ben Asher; (1269-1340); Germany; Spain
Baal Shem Tov		Rabbi Yisroel ben Eliezer; (1698-1760); Ukraine; founder of Chassidut
Bach		Rabbi Yoel ben Shmuel Sirkis; (1561-1640); Belarus; *Bayit Chadash*
Baratz	Reb Michael	Hollywood, Florida
Becher	Rabbi Mordechai	Gateways; Yeshiva University; Australia; New Jersey
Beis HaLevi		Rabbi Yosef Dov Soloveitchik; (1820-1892); Belarus
Beit Yosef		commentary on Tur; precursor to *Shulchan Aruch*; Rabbi Yosef Karo; (1488-1575); Spain; Portugal; Tzfat, Israel

Bengio	Reb Daniel	Hollywood, Florida
Ben Ish Chai		Rabbi Yosef Chaim; (1835-1909); Baghdad
Berditchever Rebbe		Rabbi Levi Yitzchak of Berditchev; (1740-1809); Ukraine; *Kedushas Levi*
Birkei Yosef		see Chida
Bnei Yissaschar		Rabbi Tzvi Elimelech Spira; (1783–1841); Munkatch, Galicia
Brisker Rav		see Rabbi Yitzchak Zev Halevy Soloveitchik
Butman	Rabbi Shmuel	Brooklyn
Caroline	Rabbi Yoel	Chabad of Key Biscayne, Florida
Chanukas HaTorah		Rabbi Avraham Yehoshua Heschel; (1595-1663); Krakow, Poland
Chasam Sofer		Rabbi Moshe Schreiber; (1762-1839); Germany; Austria
Chaver	Rabbi Yitzchak Isaac	(1789-1852); Lithuania; second generation student of the Vilna Gaon
Chida		Rabbi Chaim Yosef David Azulai; (1724-1806); Israel; Livorno, Italy
Chofetz Chaim		Rabbi Yisrael Meir Kagan; (1839-1933); Russian Empire; Radin, Poland; *Mishnah Berurah*
Ciner	Rabbi Yisroel	Beth Jacob Congregation; Irvine, California
Daat Zakainim		Collection of *Torah* commentary by various Baalei HaTosafot, disciples of Rashi; 13th century
Damesek Eliezer		Rabbi Eliezer Hager; (1890-1945); Vizhnitz, Ukraine
Davis	Rabbi Edward	Rabbi Emeritus, Young Israel of Hollywood-Fort Lauderdale; Florida
Dessler	Eliyahu Eliezer	(1892 – 1953); Gateshead, England; Bnei Brak, Israel

Divrei Yoel		Rabbi Yoel Teitelbaum; (1887-1979); Satmar Rebbe; Hungary; New York
Dubner Maggid		Rabbi Jacob ben Wolf Kranz of Dubno; (c. 1740-1804); Lithuania
Feiglin	Reb Moshe	Israeli politician; Yerushalayim, Israel
Feinstein	Rav Moshe	(1895-1986); Belarus; New York; *Igros Moshe*
Flom	Rabbi Chaim	(d. 2008); Yeshivat Ohr David; Yerushalayim, Israel
Frand	Rabbi Yissocher	Yeshivas Ner Yisroel; Baltimore
Frank	Mrs. Jamie	Eishet Chayil; Hollywood, Florida; Israel
Gilden	Rabbi Moshe Peretz	Milwaukee, Wisconsin
Greenblatt	Rabbi Ephraim	(1932-2014); Memphis; *Rivevos Ephraim*
Grundwerg	Reb Shmuel	Sammy; Miami Beach; Los Angeles; Efrat, Israel
Hahn	Reb Yossi	Hollywood, Florida
Halberstam	Rabbi Yechezkel Shraga	Stropkover Rav; (1811-1899); Poland
Hirsch	Rabbi Samson Raphael	(1808-1888); Hamburg, Germany
Iturei Torah		Reb Aharon Yaacov Greenberg; (1900-1963); Israel
Jablinowitz	Rabbi Michael	Yeshivat Ateret Yerushalayim; Israel
Jaffee	Dr. Mark	Hollywood, Florida
Jankovits	Rabbi Yossi	GIL Torah Outreach; Israel; Hollywood, Florida
Kalatsky	Rabbi Yosef	Yad Avraham Institute; New York
Kasher	Rabbi Menachem Mendel	*Torah Sheleimah*;(1895-1983); Poland; Yerushalayim, Israel
Kedushas Levi		see Berditchever Rebbe

Kelemen	Rabbi Leib	Yerushalayim, Israel
KiTov	Rabbi Eliyahu	(1912-1976); Poland; Yerushalayim, Israel
Klass	Rabbi Yaakov	Congregation K'hal Bnei Matisyahu; Brooklyn
Kli Yakar		Rabbi Shlomo Ephraim ben Aaron Luntschitz; (1550-1619); Prague
Kook	Rabbi Avraham Yitzchak	(1865-1935); Russian Empire, Palestine; First Ashkenazi Chief Rabbi of Palestine and founder of Yeshivat Merkaz HaRav
Kol Rinah		Rabbi Yitzhak ben Tzion Shapiro; 1913; Slutsk, Belarus
Kotzker Rebbe		Rabbi Menachem Mendel Morgensztern; (1787-1859); Poland
Levine	Reb Josh	Hollywood, Florida
Likutei Moharan		Rabbi Nachman of Breslov; (1772-1810); Uman, Ukraine
Lipietz	Rabbi Yitzchak	(c. 1870); Poland; *Sefer Matamim*
Lubavitcher	Rebbe	Rabbi Menachem Mendel Schneerson; (1902-1994); Ukraine; New York
Maharal		Rabbi Judah Loew ben Bezalel; (1520-1609); Prague
Maharzav / Maharzu		commentary on Midrash Rabbah; Rabbi Zev Wolf Einhorn; (d. 1862); Poland
Malbim		Rabbi Meir Leibush ben Yechiel Michel Wisser; (1809-1879); Russian Empire
Mansour	Rabbi Eli	Congregation Beit Yaakob; Brooklyn
Me'Am Loez		commentary on Tanach written in Ladino; initiated by Rabbi Yaakov Culi; (d. 1732); Turkey
Mesilat Yesharim		Rabbi Moshe Chaim Luzzatto; (1707-1746); Italy; Netherlands; Israel
Midrash HaNeelam		Rabbi Moses ben Shem Tov de Leon; (1250-1305); Spain

Midrash Rabbah		collection of *Aggadic Midrashim* on the books of the Tanach
Mishnah Berurah		see *Chofetz Chaim*
Mishneh Torah		Rambam; (1135-1204); Cordoba, Spain
Moses	Reb Aaron	Giving is Loving Chesed Fund; Hollywood, Florida
Moses	Reb Abie	legend; Hollywood, Florida
Nesivos Sholom		Rabbi Sholom Noach Berezovsky; Slonimer Rebbe; (1911 – 2000); Belarus; Yerushalayim, Israel
Neuberger	Reb Roy S.	New York
Nightingale	Rabbi Tzvi	Aish HaTorah South Florida; Hollywood, Florida
Ohr HaChaim (HaKaddosh)		Rabbi Chaim ben Moshe ibn Attar; (1696-1743); Morocco; Israel
Orach Chayim		portion of *Shulchan Aruch*
Pam	Rabbi Avraham	(1913-2001); Rosh Yeshivah of Torah V'Daas; Brooklyn
Parnes	Rabbi Moshe	Rosh Kollel; Hollywood Community Kollel; Hollywood, Florida
Pesikta d'Rav Kahane		5th or 6th century compilation of *Aggadot Midrashim* on *Shabbat* and *Chagim*
Pomerantz	Rabbi Yoel	Israel
Prero	Rabbi Yehudah	Baltimore, Maryland
Rabbeinu Bachaiya		Rabbi Bachaiya ben Asher ibn Halawa; (1255-1340); Spain
Rabinowitz	Rabbi Shmuel	Rabbi of the Kotel; Yerushalayim, Israel
Rambam		Rabbi Moshe ben Maimon; Maimonides; (1135-1204); Cordoba, Spain; *Mishneh Torah, Moreh Nevuchim*
Ramban		Rabbi Moshe ben Nachman; Nachmanides; (1194-1270); Spain

Rashi		Rabbi Shlomo Yitzchaki; (1040-1105); France
Rema		Rabbi Moshe Isserles; (1520-1572); Poland; *HaMapah*
Resnick	Rabbi Asher	Aish HaTorah; Yerushalayim, Israel
Riskin	Rabbi Shlomo	Chief Rabbi of Efrat; Founder of Ohr Torah Stone; New York; Israel
Ropshitz Rebbe		Rabbi Menachem Mendel Rubin; (c. 1740 – 1803); Ukraine
Salanter	Rabbi Yisroel	Rabbi Yisroel ben Ze'ev Wolf Lipkin; (1809-1883); Lithuania; Germany; father of the *mussar* movement
Salid	Rabbi Yitzchak	Project for the Advancement of Torah in Hollywood (PATH); Israel; Hollywood, Florida
Satmar Rav		see *Divrei Yoel*
Schachter	Rabbi Herschel	Rosh Yeshiva, Rabbi Isaac Elchanan Theological Seminary, Yeshiva University; New York
Schwab	Rabbi Shimon	(1908-1995); Germany; New York
Seder Olam Rabbah		Rabbi Yose ben Halafta; (160 C.E.)
Sefer HaRokeach		Rabbi Eliezer of Worms; (c. 1176-1238); Germany
Sefer HaToda'ah		Rabbi Avraham Eliyahu Mokotow (Eliyahu Kitov); (1912 – 1976); Poland; Israel
Sefer Yossifun		"Josefus"; Yosef ben Matityahu HaKohein; (37 - c. 100); Roman-Jewish historian; Jerusalem, Israel; Rome
Senter	Rabbi Chaim Zvi	Aderes HaTorah; Yerushalayim, Israel
Sforno		Rabbi Ovadia Ben Jacob Sforno; (1475-1550); Italy

Shapiro	Rabbi Meir	Lubliner Rav; (1887-1933); founder of *Daf Yomi*; Poland
Shelah (HaKadosh)		*Shnei Luchot HaBrit*; Rabbi Yeshaya Halevi Horowitz;(c. 1565-1630); Prague; Israel
Shem MiShmuel		Rabbi Shmuel Bornsztain; (1855-1926); Poland ; second Sochatchover Rebbe
Shulchan Aruch		Code of Jewish Law; Rabbi Yosef Karo; (1488-1575); Spain; Portugal; Tzfat, Israel
Sinclair	Rabbi Yaacov Asher	Ohr Somayach; Yerushalayim, Israel
Slonimer Rebbe		See Nesivos Shalom
Sobol	Reb Ephraim	Hollywood, Florida
Soloveitchik	Rabbi Aaron	(1917-2001); Russia; Poland; New York; Illinois
Soloveitchik	Rabbi Joseph B.	The Rav; (1903-1993); Belarus; Boston; New York; *Lonely Man of Faith*
Soloveitchik	Rabbi Yitzchak Zev Halevi	the Brisker Rav; the Gryz; (1886-1959); Belarus; Israel
Sprecher	Rabbi Ephraim	Diaspora Yeshiva; Yerushalayim, Israel
Stone	Rabbi Abraham	Congregation Adas Yeshurun; Brooklyn
Sutton	Rabbi David	Yad Yosef Torah Center; Brooklyn
Ta'amei HaMinhagim		Rabbi Avraham Yitzchak Sperling; (1851-1921); Ukraine
Targum Yonatan (ben Uziel)		Targum to the Nevi'im written in Aramaic by Rabbi Yonatan ben Uziel
Tatz	Rabbi Dr. Akiva	Jerusalem Medical Ethics Forum; South Africa; England
Torah Temimah		Rabbi Baruch Epstein; (1860-1941); Belarus

Tosafot		medieval commentaries on the Talmud; France
Turetsky	Reb Ricky	Miami Beach
Turk	Rabbi Neal	Director of Professional Rabbinics at Rabbi Isaac Elchanan Theological Seminary (RIETS), Yeshiva University; New York
Tur		*Tur Shulchan Aruch*; *Arba'ah Turim*; see Baal HaTurim
Twerski	Rabbi Dr. Abraham J.	founder of Gateway Rehabilitation Center in Pittsburgh, associate professor of psychiatry at University of Pittsburgh's School of Medicine, founder of the Shaar Hatikvah rehabilitation center for prisoners in Israel; Wisconsin; Pennsylvania; New Jersey
Tzadok HaKohen	Rabbi	Rabbi Tzadok haKohen Rabinowitz of Lublin; (1823-1913); Poland
Tzror Hamor		Rabbi Abraham Saba; (1440-1508); Iberian Peninsula; Portugal; Morocco
Vedibarta Bam		Rabbi Moshe Bogomilsky; Khal Beis Rivkah; Brooklyn
Vilna Gaon		Rabbi Eliyahu ben Shlomo Zalman Kremer; GR"A; (1720-1797); Lithuania; *Aderet Eliyahu*
Wachsman	Rabbi Ephraim	Rosh Yeshiva of Yeshivah Meor Yitzchak; Monsey, New York
Wasserstrom	Rabbi Keith	Hollywood, Florida
Wein	Rabbi Berel	Beit Knesset HaNasi; Yeshivah Ohr Sameach; Israel
Weinberg	Rabbi Yaakov	(1923-1999); Yeshivas Ner Yisroel; Baltimore

Weinberger	Rabbi Moshe	Founder or Congregation Aish Kodesh; Woodmere, New York; Mashgiach Ruchani of Rabbi Isaac Elchanan Theological Seminary, Yeshiva University; New York
Weinstock	Rabbi Yosef	Mara Datra of Young Israel of Hollywood-Fort Lauderdale, Florida
Weiss	Rabbi Avi	Hebrew Institute of Riverdale; Bronx
Weiss	Rabbi Moshe Meir	Agudas Yisroel of Staten Island; New York
Yalkut Me'Am Loez		1967 Hebrew translation of *Me'Am Loez* by Rabbi Shmuel Kravitzer
Yalkut HaMachiri		Rabbi Machir ben Abba Mari; late 13th or early 14th century *Midrash*; Provence, France
Yalkut Shemoni		early 13th century compilation of *Aggadot Midrashim* on the Tanach
Yismach Moshe		Rabbi Moshe Teitelbaum; (1759-1841); Hungary
Zohar		Kabbalistic commentary on the Torah and mysticism, thought to be written by Rabbi Moshe Shem Tov de Leon; (1250-1305); Spain; based on the writings of Rabbi Shimon Bar Yochai
Zweig	Rabbi Yochanan	Rosh Yeshivah; Yeshivah V'Kollel Beis Moshe Chaim; Miami Beach

www.ingramcontent.com/pod-product-compliance
Lightning Source LLC
Chambersburg PA
CBHW060104230426
43661CB00033B/1416/J